RISE UP OR DIE!

THE STRUGGLE AGAINST THE GENOCIDE OF BLACK PEOPLE IN BRAZIL

RISE UP OR DIE!

THE STRUGGLE AGAINST THE GENOCIDE OF BLACK PEOPLE IN BRAZIL

Andreia Beatriz Silva dos Santos, Hamilton Borges dos Santos, and João H. Costa Vargas

COMMON
NOTIONS

Brooklyn, NY
Philadelphia, PA
commonnotions.org

ISBN: 978-1-945335-28-0 | eBook ISBN: 978-1-945335-57-0
Library of Congress Number: 2025937040

10 9 8 7 6 5 4 3 2 1

Common Notions   Common Notions
c/o Interference Archive   c/o Making Worlds Bookstore
314 7th St.   210 S. 45th St.
Brooklyn, NY 11215   Philadelphia, PA 19104

www.commonnotions.org
info@commonnotions.org

Discounted bulk quantities of our books are available for organizing, educational, or fundraising purposes. Please contact Common Notions at the address above for more information.

Cover design by Josh MacPhee
Layout design and typesetting by Sydney Rainer
Printed by union labor in Canada on acid-free paper

CONTENTS

"WHEN LIBERATION KNOCKS, OPEN THE DOOR TO RISE UP, DIE, REBIRTH"

Joy James

Quantum entanglement is the concept or theory that we are all interrelated and empirically an extension of each other. This brilliant book from the perspective of Black Brazilian intellectuals and organizers instructs us on how we might fight, dance, and play within our entangled lives which are shaped by histories and destinies of Black liberation. Across (and perhaps beyond) the globe, Black people have for centuries been subjugated in ways that have made us resistors. Hence, our reactions to enslavement lead us to become architects and defenders of maroons/*quilombos*. We are the descendants of Zeferina and Harriet Tubman. Generations of mutations track centuries of rebellions: react, fight, live, die, rebirth. Our epigenetics are shaped by the torturer and the guerrilla fighter.

If we study and struggle with our lineage, we can see beyond state boundaries that countless captives and resistance fighters surveyed and survived the colonizer and plantation. We should study Rise Up or Die! as a blueprint, just as our ancestors studied the waters and landscape to map autonomy, war resistance, and to seek respite in sanctuaries. Our possibilities for fighting for freedom and autonomy are timeless. Our entanglement with love for ourselves, communities, and the natural world are endless. In the collective reactions to repressions that we have faced for centuries, we have found that despite the capture of language, culture, thought and body, our demands for freedom and autonomy have never died. So, our reactions for agency to build and protect healthy environments are more than impulses. They are lifelines from the past through the present and into the future. Hence, we always react to oppression and thus are willing in varied ways to resist or grapple with dying so that we can remain entangled within new birth—despite the violence and threats arrayed against us.

The CIA is notorious for its post-World War II assassinations, coups and covert operations against Indigenous peoples, Black populations, environmentalists, laborers, and liberators. Fugitive from enslavement and Civil War spy Harriet Tubman was finally captured by the CIA in 2022, when it chained Tubman's image into concrete. The freedom fighter stands as a statue in the CIA Quad where the Agency presents General Tubman as their loyal sentinel, as their spy because she fought for the North during the Civil War. They fail to acknowledge that Tubman—a captive maternal militant—fought for her freedom and the freedoms of Black people. In our reactions to state violence and the attempted (re)enslavement of our ancestors, we navigate varied forms of "deaths." We resist the cooptation of radical analyses and language. We provide cover for a courageous entanglement of Black militancy; one that resists sites of coercion and refuses to genuflect before police forces and corporate payouts that cripple freedom movements.

Our present struggles are tied to the past which is entangled with the future. Ancestors focused on liberation reacted and transitioned to wage freedom struggles in Africa, the Americas, Asia, and the Middle East; they fought against Western colonization. Our ancestors' reactions against repression and death revealed their familiarity with militarized and colonial police and prisons. Our ancestors have been journeying for centuries. They have entangled their desires and will into us. The ancestors have imprinted their insights and commands onto and into this book: "Rise Up or Die!" We react and/or die because we love; we also will that love into our families, communities, countries, and the world. It circulates among the ancestors, elders, adults, children, and babies. In freedom struggles, quantum entanglement is an umbilical cord pumping life into death as we resist conquest and build autonomous zones and stages of agency tied to ungendered Captive Maternals[1] engaged in caretaking, protest, mass movement, marronage, war resistance, and fortress-sanctuary.

Various reactions to repression, dishonor, humiliation and terrorism have led us to develop our spiritual resistance to physical death. We respond to myriad forms of premature and death and dying. Reading *Rise Up or Die!* evokes fidelity to liberation struggles within and beyond Brazil. Its authors comprehend the precarity of loving and living as free personas in defiance of corporate/capitalist culture and state and militia dictates. We survive as more than remnants of slavery and products purchased by predators. Even as the comprador official leadership fears resistance and stabilizes predatory policing and vampiric economics, we continue to react against antagonists who attempt to control us through capturing our ancestors.

Quantum entanglement lives within militants shaped by revolutionary love. Our inheritance and legacy reject imperialism and enslavement. Our rebellions and cultures root in Black life and death while leaping across a conceptual void that permits us to refuse to cower before conquistadores. Predators promise death. They don't control rebirth. Centuries of antiblack violence in Brazil, the US, and the Americas has allowed us to mutate into lovers and fighters while shaped by emotional, intellectual, spiritual, and material deaths and rebirths. Despite exploitation, consumption, police harassment and violence, poverty, devastation, Black agency and autonomy resists oppression. We live. We love. We react. We die. Composted into communities resisting predatory wars, we rebirth. With its critical risk-taking analyses, (auto)biographical meditations, and radical advocacies, *Rise Up or Die!* remains essentially a love story for freedom, family, culture and security and a safeguard against capture and consumption. Refusing death-by-concrete, this living text offers a gift: entanglements with our minds, hearts, fear, rage and love. Within its pages, together we study and engage fear and courage—all immersed within agape-driven resistance.

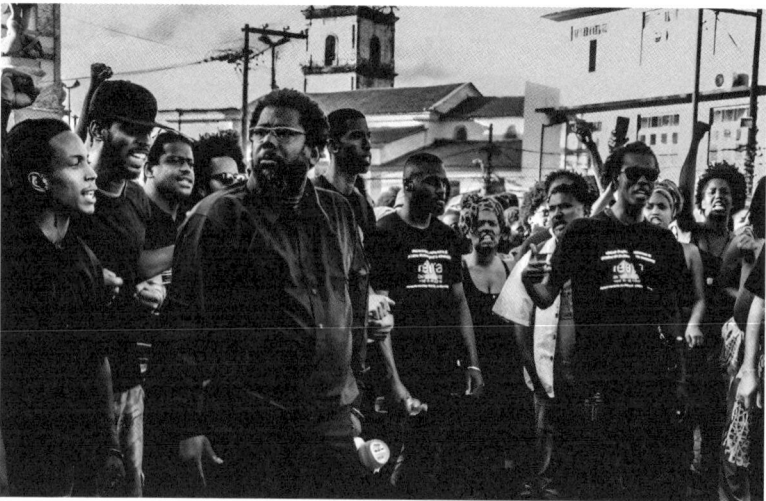

INTRODUCTION

João Costa Vargas

In 2005, Rise Up or Die! emerged in the city of Salvador, the capital of the state of Bahia, Brazil, as a campaign against the genocide of Black people.[1] Its militants professed the belief that, while there's an undeclared-but-state-sanctioned antiblack war in course—one that kills Black people physically, socially, and spiritually—to rise up is to engage in a collective reconstruction and war effort. One of Rise Up's governing premises has always been that Black communities need to rebuild themselves, strengthen their collective bonds, remember and celebrate their herstories of resistance, recognize each other, and establish structures of support and institutions through which they can not only survive the ongoing multipronged assault against their very existence, but also thrive and expand.

In its original Portuguese, the name of the organization is Reaja ou Será Morto!/Reaja ou Será Morta! While the literal translation is "React or be Killed!," in agreement with its militants we opted for "Rise Up or Die!" to emphasize the inescapable life imperative of Black mobilization the Portuguese name so forcefully conveys. Its shortened version, Reaja, which we translate as Rise Up, is also frequently used in Portuguese.

Rise Up or Die!: the name of the organization, its structure, and, more importantly, the aesthetics, ethics, and politics its militants embody, immediately suggest a state of war. Rise Up members often say, "When the police arrive, we're already practically dead." In this all-out, long-term, and lopsided battle waged against the Afro-descended by the Brazilian state and society, Black people have no choice but to mobilize and fight collectively. If they don't, they will risk dying prematurely, whether it is from police brutality, incarceration, imposed segregation, unemployment, subemployment and poverty, or from a lack of access to medication and medical facilities, medical negligence, or a constellation of widespread diseases and endemic conditions such as AIDS/HIV, diabetes, hypertension, and depression.

Andreia Beatriz Silva dos Santos, a medical doctor, Rise Up militant and one of the organization's main founders conceptualizes the persistence and ubiquity of these health and life risks as *sequela*.[2] In its most basic version, the concept of sequela suggests that, even when the immediate and initial causes of a health condition are absent, their effects remain and have an impact on individuals and their communities. The concept of sequela is a powerful analytical tool not only to make sense of current social conditions, but also to elaborate collective plans of survival and liberation.[3] Especially when it is expanded to include the adverse psychological, physical, spiritual, and collective effects of slavery on contemporary Black communities, including the post-abolition social mandate for Black people to miscegenate.[4]

Rise Up's work has been one of reconstruction, one that intends to provide means of self-defense for Black people and eventually engage in this ongoing war on a less unequal footing. As poet, writer and amateur gardener Hamilton Borges, also a militant and another one of the main founders of Rise Up generously shares, since its foundation, the organization developed support programs for incarcerated people and their families; created its own school, named after Winnie Mandela; established a book press; engaged in self-sustaining agriculture; and engendered a series of local initiatives targeting food insecurity, and mental, physical, and sexual health.

Connecting, inspiring, and receiving feedback from these concrete social actions, Rise Up holds regular meetings, seminars, and encounters that bring together multigenerational Black communities and their allies locally, nationally, and internationally. As Andreia's and Hamilton's testimonies both indicate, Rise Up's origins date back to public debates in which pressing (and often controversial) themes were openly discussed. For example, in the years preceding Rise Up's emergence, there was a weekly public event called Provocation Wednesdays in which the challenges and possibilities of the Black movement were openly debated in often heated and always well-informed exchanges.

While its militants' seemingly refractory stance relative to established Black organizations may suggest otherwise, Rise Up is firmly rooted in the contemporary Black movement—"movement" understood as the constellation of Black organizations that, since the onset of slavery in Brazil in the sixteenth century has been resisting and fighting against the dehumanization and brutalization of Black people.

Specifically, Rise Up is grounded in the main expression of the contemporary Black movement, the Movimento Negro Unificado (MNU, United Black Movement), founded in 1978 following a two-thousand people public manifestation in Brazil's largest city, São Paulo, during the military dictatorship.[5]

A longtime member of MNU, Hamilton brought an unflinching commitment to Black people's liberation to Rise Up. While Andreia was not a member of MNU, her life-long development of and dedication to a Black-centered medical practice drew from and expanded the Black movement's vision. Departing from earlier Black political formations, particularly the Frente Negra Brasileira (FNB, Brazilian Black Front) of the 1930s, MNU explicitly rejected the ideology of racial democracy, which denies the existence of antiblack racism as a constitutive and structural aspect of Brazilian society.[6] Instead, the MNU called for a "new society" in which past and present racial injustices were recognized and remedied by appropriate public policy.

Yet—and this is a critical difference on which Andreia and Hamilton expand in the pages that follow—rather than a "new society" in which, as MNU had it, "everyone participates," Rise Up's new society is a Black quilombo, an autonomous and self-sustained maroon-like state in which Black people, and particularly dark-skinned Black people, develop their own laws, modes of production, sustainable relation with the environment, African spiritual practices, and project their vision of the future.[7] This theme is given a compelling fictional literary treatment in Hamilton's recently published *Bantu Machine*, which describes a likely near future in which Black people, in the midst of apocalyptic planetary degradation, are killed without penalty within the official city confines, yet find refuge and regeneration in a high-walled, self-sustained, industrialized and environmentally-conscious quilombo.[8]

The topics of skin tone and one's degree of blackness are predictably controversial, particularly among Black people, as are the accusations of essentialism against those who dare to bring them up. Many, if not most, Black movement members and organizations have adopted the perspective on who's Black as resulting from self-declaration, which includes the entire spectrum from dark-skinned to light-skinned Black people. This perspective matches the one adopted by scholars of racial dynamics as well as the Brazilian Institute of Geography and Statistics (IBGE) that conducts the census, defining as Black the sum of those who self-identify via the color categories *preta/o* (black) and *parda/o* (brown, or mixed). The 2022 Brazilian census found that the total Black population constitutes a majority in Brazil, comprising 55.5 percent. This number includes self-identified browns who make up 45.3 percent (surpassing whites for the first time since 1872) of the total, and blacks who constitute 10.2 percent (doubling between 1991 and 2022).[9]

Rise Up welcomes light-skinned Black people into their ranks (whites are only accepted as allies and collaborators), yet its militants insist on the plethora of disadvantages experienced by dark-skinned Black people vis-à-vis their light-skinned counterparts. In doing so, they demand more precise analyses of racism, antiblackness, public health, and public policies. Most of Rise Up members are dark-skinned (the state of Bahia has the greatest concentration of pretos in the country, comprising 22.4 percent of its population), and their personal and collective experience, as well as their focused study, indicate the need to grasp the specificities of their collective experiences.

Rise Up makes a compelling case for moving beyond the accurate findings that show there are great differences in life chances between pretos and pardos, on the one hand, and whites on the other. For example, levels of homicide and poverty for pretos and pardos are similar (while both are still higher than those for whites);[10] and the same is true for food insecurity, in which condition pretos and pardos are overrepresented, while whites are underrepresented.[11] Yet educational attainment indices for pretos are measurably worse than for both pardos and whites.[12] Similar finer analyses in the areas of public health, criminal justice, housing, and exposure to environmental toxins, among others, are critical for a nuanced comprehension of Black people's experiences in relation to their appearance. Rise Up members consistently demonstrate a willingness to familiarize themselves with the theoretical and analytical tools and to think beyond the available demographic data.

Rise Up's most generative (and perhaps defining) characteristic is the feedback loop it enables between its serious study of historical developments, current social trends, and relevant social theorists (particularly Black and Pan-Africanist authors); its collective performance and public protest; its concrete social projects and interventions (such as the Winnie Mandela school, cooperative banks, and community gardens); its regular publications (books, commentaries, essays); and its vision of the future. A constantly replenished back-and-forth between practice, theory, and creative fiction: this fluidity is a powerful generator of new vocabularies, desires, and dreams—it is a fruitful enabler of invention.

Rise Up's commitment to invention as a tool of Black survival and liberation is informed by an African spirituality that refuses the separation between the physical (including the natural world) and the metaphysical (including the deceased, the not-yet-dead, and the not-yet-born). Invention, in Frantz Fanon's perspective, is the means by which our current social and ontological existence must be transfigured.[13] Rise Up members are relentless in their pursuit of invention. In this book, the reader will encounter the unremitting search for new ideas, experiments, and interventions that recognize the inescapable need to come together and transform the terms of our existence.

Sometimes this pursuance of freedom requires expansion: that's when Rise Up activists traveled all over Brazil, the Americas, Europe, and Africa. Other times, it requires an intentional retraction, which is an attempt to regroup, a search for safety, and a refusal to participate in public events. For example, in November 2024, Rise Up called for its militants and supporters to begin a "period of tactical silence": a cessation of all its public statements and direct actions so that, "based on a profound analysis of the national and international scenarios, a path towards liberation can be elaborated." While Rise Up's ongoing communitarian projects continue, their decision to remain silent was, as their social media indicated, "a means of reorienting ourselves in an unfavorable and violent context, which has been constant in our lives. Silence is not the end."

Why the imperative of invention, of replacing the terms of our existence on this planet? Because either those terms are rejected and transformed, or Black people will routinely and without scandal continue to die in multiple ways of multiple causes. To interrupt and replace this state of normality is the precondition of Black survival.

As Andreia and Hamilton painfully illustrate, particularly when they narrate their childhood—Andreia in Porto Alegre, the capital city of Rio Grande do Sul, the whitest of Brazilian states; Hamilton in Salvador, the capital city of Bahia, the state with the greatest concentration of Black people outside the African continent—the modern concept of the Human expels Black people from the human family.[14] Black people are forcefully represented as inferior, ugly, not belonging, or dangerous. At best, invisible and irrelevant. This cultural mandate's symbolism and social consequences are not only powerful and all-encompassing, they're also, for the same reasons, mostly uncontested, and internalized even by Black people raised in nurturing and critical environments. The Human is parasitic on Black people, quite literally consuming Black people and in the process reinforcing their imposed nonhumanity.[15]

Since its foundation, differently than most actors within the Black movement or progressive circles, Rise Up has insisted on the concept of genocide to describe and denounce the multifaceted, ubiquitous, foundational, and ongoing onslaught of Black people in Brazil. Genocide against Black people, they claim, is a defining characteristic of the Brazilian social formation. As one of Rise Up activists states: "Genocide is the public policy that founded and still structures the Brazilian society. The total annihilation of Black People: that is the basis of colonial states."[16] While the concept of genocide as defined by the United Nations in 1948 does not require the total elimination of a people, it points to an ideal future without Black people, in relation to which contemporary forms of violent and nonviolent exclusion gain meaning and justification.

On the non-physically-violent forms of genocide, Abdias do Nascimento argues that in Brazil and indeed in the Black diaspora, Black people are often asked to miscegenate, to "purify" their blood, which means not only to deny and condemn their current presence by seeking lighter-skinned partners and non-black environments, but also to construct a future—by willingly participating in their own erasure—in which their bodily, cultural, spiritual, and political legacy simply no longer exist.[17] The objective of the contemporary war is a nonblack future. It signals that Black people don't belong in this present time, and, in time, will be eliminated. For Rise Up activists, Brazil's purported embrace of racial democracy, according to which race-mixing is presented as a positive social trait and character disposition, is a powerful ideological farce that hides and furthers the mundane and deadly assaults on Black people. The alleged racial democracy heaven, they claim, is really an antiblack state of war.

Thus, while the ubiquitous and systematic physical death of Black people, particularly but not exclusively by the state, expresses this racial purification project in its most naked form, the genocidal assault is also microscopic, individualized, subtle, and insidious. Together, the large-scale and the microscopic processes establish a reign of genocidal brutality and terror. As Rise Up militants frequently experience—and revolt against— Black people are often told to calm down, behave properly and rationally, act in good faith, and be thankful for their station in life. Such acts of social policing are also performed by Black people who find Rise Up's approach too brash. In myriad and compounded ways, these and related directives, which derive from a foundational hatred of the Afro-descended firmly planted in the national collective conscious and unconscious, contribute to Black people's social, physical, spiritual, and ontological death.[18] This book can be read as Rise Up's relentless engagement with this genocidal context: its analysis, strategies, setbacks, alternatives, and visions of the future.

It is therefore unsurprising that Hamilton and Andreia reflect at length on both the internalized hatred Black people inevitably experience and the necessary affirming strategies of collective care and love towards and by dark-skinned Black people. Although it can be paralyzing and generate a host of negative sequelae on one's body, psyche, and of course one's social environment, hatred can be transformed into a tool of protest, creativity, and political energy. In a generative dialogue with Audre Lorde's concept of anger, creative hatred is presented as a personal and collective strategy with which to confront fear and oblivion in a context of antiblack genocide.[19] As Hamilton puts it, "creative hatred is what makes you build new things, as we've done in the last seventeen years. We've been confrontational, and we don't respect institutions. We call out white people's hatred towards us, we externalize the hatred that we've been subjected to." Andreia puts it succinctly: "There's no negotiation, there's nothing to offer except the hatred of which we are the object."[20]

The many uses of creative hatred—and indeed a plethora of daring and therefore controversial positions—mark Rise Up or Die! Its militants adopt a fearless, outspoken, and often loud stance that is unencumbered by norms of decorum, respectability, political party affiliation, or ideological persuasion. As historical Black activist Luiza Bairros remarked, Rise Up invented bad manners in Black politics.[21] Such is the imperative of invention.

Rise Up can be placed on the far-left of the political spectrum (insofar as, in theory at least, and when conditions are favorable, they're in favor of engaging in all-out warfare against the Brazilian state), and its members have been critical of left political formations that seek to reform the state and society. Rise Up militants understand that the foundational and normative requirement of Black people's imposed fungibility and a-humanity cannot be attenuated. The Workers' Party (Partido

dos Trabalhadores, PT) leftist federal administrations that gov-
erned Brazil between 2003–2016, and again since 2023, have
shown that, even when leftist public policy targets social inequal-
ity—instituting affirmative action in universities and government
occupations, as well as lifting more than fifty million people out
of poverty—Black people continue to die disproportionately. The
point is made evident when we consider that while homicides
and police killings decreased in Brazil between 2002–2010, in this
same period these numbers went up for Black people.

Rise Up is critical of Black people and organizations as they
engage or inhabit the state machinery (whether at the local, state,
or federal levels), private national and international foundations,
and universities. It must be pointed out that Rise Up members
currently transit in those spaces or have done so in the past. For
example, many of its militants are college students, and some
of its supporters are university staff and professors. In the past,
Rise Up supported candidates running for office, but once its
critique of the electoral process and of funding practices crys-
tallized, it stopped doing so. The core of Rise Up's critique—
not unlike that raised in some progressive circles in the US—is
that the electoral process, foundations, and universities are so
immersed in their own dynamics of power, knowledge production and reproduction, prestige, and resources, that they operate
against the interests of the most vulnerable people—paradoxically
the very population that elected representatives, state operatives
and bureaucrats, organizers, and academics claim to support.[22]

Rise Up recuperates the radical critique of Black movement
dissidents such as Yedo Ferreia who considered the MNU core,
including members of related Black formations such as Insti-
tuto de Pesquisas das Culturas Negras (IPCN, Black Cultures
Research Institute), the "elite of the elite." Ferreira parted ways
with the MNU based on what he saw as a fundamental difference
in positions: whereas the members' consensus defined MNU as a
revindication movement, Ferreira and other dissidents wanted it
to be a mobilization formation.[23] Rise Up takes up an orientation

similar to Ferreira's, and squarely defines itself in terms of permanent and necessary mobilization, embracing constant experimentation, allowing for expansion and retraction, and always dreaming of a Black autonomous future, not an integrated future.

It is important to heed Rise Up's critique of institutionalized regimes of knowledge and power—even the supposedly progressive—because it helps us to ask questions about what type of organizing is the most effective for Black lives. Providing contours of a collective practice that centers autonomous knowledge production, and recognizes in formations of state and empire the centrality of antiblackness, Rise Up proposes a type of permanent mobilization rooted in Black study. As a verb, and as an activity that is carried out in permanent dialogue, research, and experimentation, Black study embraces Black people's survival. Indeed, Black survival, because it categorically negates the logic of the Brazilian empire-state, necessitates a truly revolutionary approach. Hence the imperative of invention.[24]

As will become evident in Andreia and Hamilton's reflections, Rise Up and its members have given up on Brazil. They don't believe in the state and society's willingness and capacity to integrate Black people; as individuals and as a people they affirm they don't belong, that their citizenship is a farce. This stance goes hand-in-hand with their forced expulsion from the Human family. If they are not considered human, why would they be considered citizens? More pragmatically, by renouncing their country of birth, they reject the illusion of integration and participation in Brazil's so-called civil society. A tangible example of this revolt against the illusion of integration and citizenship, particularly as it concerns the rejection of political institutions and the democratic process itself, was the 2016 campaign "Don't Vote, Rise Up!" Here, again, this directive parallels MNU dissident militants who, particularly between 1977 and 1980, insisted on publishing essays and pamphlets, making a robust case against participation in elections.[25] Of note is that in Brazil the vote is mandatory for all adults. Calling for a rejection of the electoral process amounts to mass civil and legal disobedience. In doing so, it makes its similarities with dissenting voices of the contemporary Black movement and with Rise Up's serious critique of Brazilian democracy evident, linking it to the modern planetary-defining exclusion of Black people—an exclusion that is foundational, ubiquitous, and enduring.[26]

Given the abundant employment of creative hatred in Rise Up's activities, particularly in protests against the murderous state apparatus, it is perhaps surprising that another central, if not dominant, element of their daily practice is Black love. In the always direct and honest dialogues, as in the consistently welcoming, protective, generous, and abundant and multifaceted support one receives in Rise Up, Black love figures prominently. The proximity—indeed the familiarity—with death, another Rise Up facet Andreia and Hamilton bigheartedly describe, ironically demonstrates time and time again its unconditional support of victims of the ongoing antiblack war.

Providing immediate moral, financial, juridical, and political assistance to the interminable victims' families, Rise Up militants, particularly Andreia and Hamilton, often against their own best interests of health and financial stability, show up at the sites of the latest assassination; help identify the bodies at the Coroner's Office; assist in the filling of endless paperwork; mediate conversations with state official, lawyers, and a gamut of bureaucrats; and contribute decisively to providing mortuary services that are dignified. It is small wonder that, after decades of being immersed in these macabre rituals, Hamilton now declares that he needs a break. Whereas he previously described himself as an amateur gravedigger, he now presents himself as an amateur gardener.

Black love extends to and defines the ongoing seminars, book talks, a variety of classes that take place at the Winnie Mandela school—including boxing, an old dream of Hamilton—as well as in the daily work at the state of Bahia's main prison, where Andreia had her practice between 2007–2023. Black love orients the organized conversations on sexuality and gender that allow women and men of various sexual orientations to share their vulnerabilities, perceive their mistakes, and support each other. It was in one of those men's circles—whose genealogy Hamilton links to the MNU women's critique of its internal and constitutive heteropatriarchy—where a Black transgender woman felt safe to announce her transition.

Rise Up's own version of Quilombismo, adapted from the works of Abdias do Nascimento and Beatriz Nascimento (no relation), translates Black love into a detailed blueprint of an alternative social formation that is protected and protecting. Autonomous, based on self-defense, and economically self-sufficient, the Rise Up quilombo is a project of and for the future. While it rejects the nation and the state in whose legal territory it is established, its focus is on recuperating and reinventing African traditions of spirituality, sociality, justice, well-being, and sustainable and respectful relations with the natural world. Inspired by the uncompromising spirit of Zeferina, the nineteenth-century African woman warrior of the Urubu quilombo in Salvador, the Rise Up quilombo does not ask for anything. It establishes itself and provides a loving refuge for those whose lives, outside of it, are worthless. As vividly imagined in Hamilton's *Bantu Machine,* in Rise Up's quilombista utopia, which expresses the imperative of invention, the newly arrived find an immediate, although at first disorienting (because unthought of), safe heaven that is extremely well organized:

> [All newcomers] are astonished at what they see. People in light clothes produced in the quilombista factories, colorful clothes, the same colors that cover the surrounding buildings, the grandiose paintings, statues, and gigantic murals, a bit of art in every part of the immense central square, animals that they thought were extinct pass by the crowd. In the distance, soldiers on mighty horses and each carrying a high-powered rifle, wear impeccable liberation army uniforms; they're the rebels that protect the sacred city.

It's not often that you get a close look at the liberation army in such concentration. Today is a special day, a day to celebrate freedom and worship the waters, the throne of waters. The quilombista fortress is real.[27]

As much as collective dreams of liberation are also calls for invention and concrete action, Rise Up's quilombista dream is indeed real and already happening.

*

What follows is based on more than seventy hours of conversations recorded between July 2022 and January 2023 in which Andreia and Hamilton discussed, from their personal and collective perspectives, Rise Up's origins, development, guiding principles, distinct phases, and visions of the future. I edited, rearranged, and translated the conversations, and while Andreia and Hamilton were generous in answering my follow-up questions, particularly about dates, places, and names, all errors are mine.

CHAPTER ONE

BEGINNINGS

Hamilton and Andreia reflect on formative moments of their personal trajectories leading up to the formation of Rise Up or Die!

INTIMACY WITH DEATH

João: Hamilton, can you please reflect about your personal experiences that prepared you for the emergence of Rise Up?

Hamilton: I was born in a family dominated by women. As I grew up, they surrounded me with a vast inventory of ancestral and spiritual explanations. I have an ancestral mark, from my initiation in Candomblé, which is that I was born with the dead.[1] It's a choice that I made before I was born. I discovered this along my life trajectory.

This is the first thing I have to mention in terms of being prepared for the struggle: the close relationship with death. I've always had that, but I only noticed it in Rise Up or Die! That's why, when we are at a protest march, we say, "Look behind us, you'll see the dead." About five years after Rise Up started, the police killed a young mother while she was carrying her baby; she was shot in the back of the head. Immediately upon hearing about it, we went to the scene. We arranged buses. We had about two hundred people. The police claimed we had fifty, we said we had five thousand. We said, "You're not counting the dead."

My grandmother and my maternal aunts raised me. Like all men in my family, my father disappeared. The men are away from home, they're not working. They show up only every now and then; they drink; they're in trouble. Such are the men in my family. But women are present and in my family they're very strong. I see this from today's perspective. My mother was a child when she had me: she was only fourteen when she had the first child and I was born when she was sixteen; my father was already forty or so. When I was born, my maternal grandfather and my mother's family all left because they thought the situation was unacceptable. My grandmother then forced my father to marry my mother. A lot of drama as you can imagine. Women told men what to do, and there was never a man in control. In my family, women don't control things behind the scenes; they do it directly and openly.

There's a person in my family, my great-grandmother Guiomar, whom I constantly think about as a reference. We have nothing in writing, only stories. She was originally from Nazaré das Farinhas [state of Bahia] but moved to Salvador, to São Gonçalo, where she was an Ekedi in a Candomblé house.[2] She took over a large bush area that belonged to the Companhia União Fabril [a chemicals corporation]. União Fabril was originally a slave trade company, and it owned the central area of Salvador that today is Liberdade. My great-grandmother paid to stay on that land, and União Fabril charged us, like, one Real. My great-grandmother had only one daughter, light skinned, so my great-grandmother could have been raped. This daughter, my grandmother, hated light-skinned people. If you dated someone light-skinned, she'd say, "Don't even bring this person here."

Guiomar met the great love of her life, Dona Vanju, and they were together for over fifty years. Dona Vanju is a fundamental part of my family's story. My family was entrepreneurial. My great grandmother rode horses, she wore pants, she had a bodyguard named Manoel. She was known as a *partido alto* woman, which is what lesbians were called back then. She'd stab others, she had a gun; she worked in a white family's house; her employers liked her. From that white family, she'd bring back a lot of clothes, silverware, and food. Every year, she'd have a big party for her partner, and the party lasted seven days. It was decorated with little flags, it had samba musicians, it was a party she'd give to celebrate the love of her life.

This impacted me deeply because my great grandmother forged an idea in our family that we were a tough and fearless people. We weren't hearing this from men; we were hearing this from women. My father was a wonderful musician but he could not get adjusted in life. The men showed up for some of the parties and then would disappear again. I grew up seeing this. If someone mistreated you, they'd have to contend with all these women (and the men they'd drag along). My family, the Borges, and the Machado family were both strong, so much so that we were advised to never fight with the Machados. I remember I had a fight with a Machado that almost had me drowned in the sewer. My folks said, "It's better to leave it alone; or, you can fight with him, but we adults cannot get involved because we may have deaths." So no one messed with the Borges and the Machados.

I was raised in an environment that was like a maroon. Dirt roads, a lot of bush, there were cows, and a tram line that longshoremen and other people used. Our land was almost collective land because we had a lot of it, and many families planted on it. We had a well, and many people fetched water from it.

We also had something Andreia talks about, which I think is the same anywhere Black people live: if I was caught smoking weed, someone would scold me and take me home. It was an extended family, everyone took care of everyone else. We were often out in the streets; the streets were ours, there wasn't this notion that you had to avoid the streets. We'd do our homework at home, but we'd play, we'd steal mangoes, and we'd steal little things. That was my childhood. It was a difficult childhood because I began to walk very late—I had a bunch of development problems, and my brother had to carry me everywhere. It also took me a long time to learn how to read and write; I couldn't learn like the other kids.

I grew up observing the women in my family: praying, organizing parties. Those women took care of other women and they were very respected, including by the outlaws. I remember this one person who was on a hit list, my friend César Caruso. The killer was going to be Seu Nadinho, who was waiting in front of our house. My grandmother opened the window and said, "What are you up to, Nadinho?" That moment allowed César to run away. She was the matriarch of the entire community. She had a lot of power. Everyone asked for her blessings.

Inside my neighborhood, Curuzu, I was protected. The problems that Andreia had because she was in majority-white spaces [we will see shortly], I never had. I've never felt ugly. I never found a woman like Andreia ugly. My first girlfriend—I must have been fourteen—she looked like Andreia: the skin tone, the manners. In Curuzu everyone was proud to be Black, everyone was proud of their traditions.

But then I grew up and I got to know the streets of the city. Only then I discovered Salvador. I started going downtown, to Pelourinho. There were sex workers; there were drugs. I'd go to Pituba, where there were white-majority parties. People would beat us in Pituba. In Curuzu, we always had the ocean nearby, but as a teenager I wanted to have the swimming pool experience. So my friends and I climbed the walls of private clubs and jumped in the pool. Then the guards would catch us and lock us up until 6 p.m., when everyone left, and they'd make us do their job for them, cleaning the entire pool and collecting the chairs. We'd come back from Pituba walking because it was Sunday and there weren't buses running. That's when I began noticing racism more intensely, even though we were very protected inside our neighborhood.

In the 1980s, the death squad of the police was called Grupo Especializado em Prevenção, Perda, e Eventos (Group Specialized in Prevention, Loss, and Events, GEPPE). Today, there's a debate about genocide or extermination, but since my childhood I've known genocide quite well from personal experiences. I had to protect myself from those constant dangers. We didn't have this thing about carrying our IDs, like it was for Andreia. We only got our IDs when we turned eighteen. But we didn't go to places where we knew the police were killing people. Dead bodies would show up all the time; the Civil Police had blue cars; there were radio programs that talked about Mão Branca, a hitman, probably a police officer, who killed many young Black people.

Since I was a kid I've been familiarized with the narratives about extermination; I heard them in bars, I heard them in my grandmother's advice: "Be careful, don't hang out with certain folks." But I ended up doing just the opposite, and hanging out with people who made me more vulnerable. I don't like talking about this, but I've seen a lot. My friends were arrested and they talked about what prison was like. When I was arrested, I already understood the incarcerated people's predicament. And I knew there was something wrong—I knew it was related to the color of our skin. I promised myself that one day I'd come back to prison as a lawyer. I ended up coming back as an activist of Rise Up or Die!

THEATER AND "OS MALOQUEIROS"

Hamilton: In the early 1980s, we lost the União Fabril land. My grandmother and my aunt were getting old and they couldn't stop others from occupying the land. The main house was destroyed and we became very poor. I decided to not be a burden to my family. There were people who wanted me and my brother dead. I thought I'd die at seventeen. The threat came from other Black people. I couldn't stay any longer in the neighborhood where I was born and where I lived.

In the neighborhood there was a teacher who was very compassionate—the type that takes care of everyone. When he saw me imitating Ney Matogrosso,[3] and lip-syncing his songs, he said I should do theater at the SENAC.[4] I was destitute, and the neighborhood was now awful: there were no brick houses, no asphalt, no water—we'd drink water from a fountain. I thought that theater was the same thing as dance. I had heard about a lot of people from my community traveling to Europe on dance tours. I tried theater because the audition seemed easier: I had to recite a poem and sing a song.

It took me four tries to get into the SENAC program. Sônia de Brito was the director, Milton Gomes the vice-director. The theater school was majority white. (By the way, I'm going there again this week, after thirty years, I'm very moved.) Sônia, a white woman, told me I was emotionally unstable. At that time, I was a boy coming out of hell: I didn't have proper shoes, I didn't know how to express myself. The emotional instability that they saw in me was my blackness.

In 1986, I finally passed the test and enrolled in the SENAC theater course. For the audition, I sang an Ilê Ayê song and recited a poem by Elis Regina.[5] I think I only got in because they felt sorry for me. The course included set building and everything that was involved in the production of theater plays. It was then that I learned how to read; I already liked poetry and singing. Later, I also completed a cooking course inside SENAC.

My first honest salary was inside the theater. SENAC paid a stipend for each spectacle, and I did four spectacles per month. I was very dedicated. I studied and I got good at it. I also did well in the cooking course. Compared to my neighborhood Curuzu, I saw myself in another context, another way of talking, dressing, I was surrounded by artists. I was all day at SENAC: I arrived at 7 a.m., attended cooking class, had lunch, rested for a couple of hours, and then worked on the theater shows. My first theater show was Silio Boccanera Junior's *O Meio do Mundo* (The Middle of the World). I was the devil. At that time, the Pelourinho neighborhood was not as hip as it is today; it was a zone of prostitution, and it was considered unsafe. I was there every day for about five years, and I made some money.

Later, I started staying at my theater friends' houses; in turn, they stayed in my Candomblé house, where I was initiated. I changed completely. So much so that when I returned to Curuzu, I had black lipstick and black clothing, which was something we all did at the theater. Corumbá, a person at Curuzu who was supposed to be the toughest one around, was trying to mock my masculinity because of what I was wearing and said he'd kill me. My brother, who was also known to be a tough guy, told me I should fight Corumbá otherwise he would beat me every time he saw me. So I had to fight him.

I've met both very affectionate and very tough people in my life. The same is true for my family. We had to be tough; I had friends who were violent, and friends who were loving, who knew how to have fun. Only in the theater did I start to be more playful. My social life became centered on the theater, and that's how I reshaped my life. I learned different acting and production techniques, and I became someone respected and important in that environment. I felt relevant. The theater was crucial for me because it opened up the possibility of a life outside Curuzu.

I constantly questioned race and race relations. Even though white people were a minority in my theater circles, they were more valued than we Black people. I challenged that, and often

I got into arguments. Luiza Bairros once gave a talk at SENAC, and I got agitated, shouting things I had learned from Malcolm X. Luiz Bandeira, a friend, had introduced me to Malcolm X by reading his book to me. Later, I dated a person from the US who also read Malcolm X for me—I found a light via Malcolm X, and it helped me find the Movimento Negro Unificado (MNU). In the MNU there were many college people and many people from the base [the grassroots]. I was a Black person from the base. The college people were very eloquent whereas we, the *maloqueiros* from the base, were more ghetto and forged a different, more angry, political perspective. For us, anger was not a bad thing. Quite the opposite: we were angry at racism and we embraced the anger. We started many community projects, which is something I learned from my great grandmother and my grandmother: I observed how they dialogued with people and built things with them. Then I learned more from MNU and we started to form *núcleos de base*, base nuclei, in several communities.

That's how I found myself. I knew theater, I knew how to cook, and I was part of the movement. I started to read abundantly. Everyone had to read up on particular authors or books and get ready for the Sunday debates. On Saturday, I'd get up at five in the morning to join the *curso de formação,* a formation course in which activists taught each other. Sometimes it was someone my age, but this person would be in college, so they'd have more information than I did. There was respect for the information this person shared. All this was crucial: people who went through the courses liked libraries and often started libraries.

I have a friend, Renílson, who teaches boxing and is about four years older than me; when I met him, he was nineteen, like an adult for me at the time. He started several libraries and he was the first person who gave me a book, Nietzsche's *Thus Spoke Zarathustra*. We had a dream of one day having a boxing academy in the same building as a library. This dream has come true: in the Rise Up or Die! building we have a library and we teach boxing.

The Black movement made this dream come true; Renílson made it come true. He didn't smoke weed, he didn't steal. He had a group who arranged fights in the streets. He was a fighter. If you smoked weed or you stole, you were out of the group. I was kicked out of the group.

Theater was fundamental. You see, at that moment in my life I felt like a failure because I didn't have the things the majority of people my age had because I had opted to live instead of staying in the world of crime. If I stayed, I would have died. I didn't have shoes, I didn't have clean clothes, hip clothes, but I was alive. And then theater happened: to act, to study theater, to be part of a play and hear applause, that was all I cared for. I actually made some decent money between 1986–1988 because theater provided stipends. I'd conceptualize the plays, rehearse them, and I became part of the SENAC leadership. I wasn't a registered worker, but I had money. Sônia de Brito was fundamental for me, because she was strict and she demanded a lot from me. She insisted that I speak correctly and only based on information. She'd often say, "You can't opine about this matter because you haven't studied it."

In 1989, I started a poetry slam group called Os Maloqueiros (The Ghetto People)—we were very poor, we were from the periphery neighborhoods. There was a Black, somewhat middle-class, intelligentsia in the city—people who today are prominent in the formal political world, and they were already prepared for that trajectory. We were maloqueiros, and my knowledge of theater gave me tools and weapons to develop my own role in the Black movement. We had cultural groups inside the communities: we produced plays and involved the local people. But we had no fancy clothes or shoes; we wore sandals instead. The middle class people pejoratively called us maloqueiros. We adopted that word and we made it ours, just like the Black movement had adopted the word *negro*, and used it as a weapon.

We participated in many events around the centenary of abolition in Brazil [which happened in 1988]. Paul Simon came to the Pelourinho, where he met singer Margaret Menezes and the group Olodum. That's when the gentrification of Pelourinho began—white people started to move in and buy houses, and the government started pushing poor people out of the neighborhood to far away areas. Os Maloqueiros confronted the gentrifying white people. We'd say, "The movement is Black Soul, Black Soul, Black Soul!" We'd proclaim loudly, "Check it out, check it out, a sale from the Military Police Shock Troop: have a shotgun candy and set up a date with the devil!"[6] When we'd see a *gringo,* we'd shout, "Gringo, gringo, gringo!" We were young and enraged. There were many receptions downtown, and we'd crash those posh events. We'd get a bunch of food, carry it in our folded shirts, in our pockets. We'd get on the table and recite something, before security would push us out or call the police. I can't imagine doing that today. Back then, the police would come and slap us on the back of the head and tell us to leave. One time, as we were running away from the police, we asked if we could get shelter at a Workers' Party event.

João: Can you say more about the Workers' Party?

Hamilton: We hated the party's white people. Most people I knew in the Black movement thought the same. It sounds incredulous today, but people changed their perspective. When I was in the MNU, we'd say our presence in the Workers' Party was a tactic, and the party did not represent our program. The Workers' Party was not our strategy; our objective was to create the basis for a national liberation organization, and the Workers' Party was not going to do that for Black people, we had to do it ourselves. The Workers' Party was part of a tactic to enter the political establishment and have a voice in the parliament.

People who used to think that way, today say they changed, they matured. It seems like I won't mature, because I don't believe the Workers' Party was formed with Black liberation in mind. Luiza Bairros, for example, tried to be state representative in 1984, unsuccessfully. She noticed racism inside the Workers'

Party and left. I was never in the Workers' Party. In Rise Up, we even gave up the notion that Black people can have a positive impact in that type of electoral structure. Since 1986, during the debates about the new constitution, we've been saying the same things: "Don't kill Black people," "We want better health care for Black people," or "We want power for Black people." It's been almost forty years and nothing has changed.

In Rise Up, I learned that Quilombismo was the most successful experience of Black liberation. Unlike Abdias do Nascimento's perspective, we don't think we should negotiate or ask for our liberation. We've been trying to negotiate for a long time and it hasn't worked: the police are not going to stop killing us. I've learned a lot, not only from MNU, but also from my family. My great grandmother took over land, which she defended on a horse and with arms. She had a group of people helping her, also armed and on horseback. It's better to take than to ask for crumbs. The Maloqueiros was an explosion of creativity. It doesn't exist anymore, but it gave us visibility, some notoriety.

João: How long did the Maloqueiros last?

Hamilton: By 1990 I don't think we were meeting anymore. We were a very active group, we distributed food, and we had people come together to discuss their reality. We didn't have money, we didn't have anything. We had the will and wanted to change the world, but we had all kinds of difficulties: we got depressed and were brutalized by the police.

But we still saw each other. When there was an event, we were asked to do some spoken word, but we never managed to get a place to meet regularly. We didn't get a chance to publish a book with our work; no one showed us how to do it. I only published my first book when I was fifty years old because no one from among those who had already published thought about helping me out. No one said, "You're a poet, you should publish. Here's what you need to do." I thought I'd never publish. It seemed all so complicated. But when we discovered it was simple, we started publishing intensely. Now we want to make our books available to incarcerated people, we want them to publish. Our publishing house only publishes from impoverished Black people who are creative.

João: What readings impacted you?

Hamilton: Among others, *O Negro Revoltado* by Abdias do Nascimento and *Sociologia do Negro Brasileiro* by Clovis Moura. I had difficulty with the readings. Words I didn't know, I looked up. Sometimes I was embarrassed. People would laugh at me, say sly things when I didn't know how to pronounce a word in English or French. Eventually, I lost all shame, and I found many wonderful people who supported me. I memorized passages. All these bits and pieces of information eventually made sense to me and helped me forge my own ideas.

I wanted to understand my condition of being constantly discriminated against, that's why I was determined to study hard, to read extensively—I learned I had to be constantly reading a book. Even though I hadn't entered college through its admission test, I audited classes at the College of Philosophy, especially the ones Ronaldo Barros taught.

In 1993, at the SENUN—Seminário Nacional de Universitários Negros (National Seminar of Black Scholars), which took place at the Federal University of Bahia—I presented a paper on theater practice. By then I'm feeling intellectually and critically competent. I could dialogue with college people, with scholars and I became the event's coordinator even though I was not in college. I had very little formal education—I only went to school again after I met Andreia, and I managed to go to college, thanks to her. That SENUN was very important because the majority of Black activists and researchers that are relevant today were at that event, including the minister of Women, Family and Human

Rights, Nilma Lino Gomes, who has a dissertation on the Black movement as an educator,[7] which I frequently reference publicly.

The MNU also had its own courses, which were wonderful. They prepared you to speak in public, they taught you how to oppose an argument and how to debate. Because of that, I never had any problem speaking in public. I've had many debates with the most accomplished academics, and I was able to articulate my own perspective. A core objective of the MNU militants was to form new cadres, and they formed me for sure.

João: Am I understanding correctly that when Os Maloqueiros disbanded you began to be more involved with the MNU?

Hamilton: I joined the MNU a bit before the end of Os Maloqueiros. At first I didn't speak up in meetings. There were lots of university people, and I would be embarrassed to speak. When I started I never stopped—that's when I felt more structured. In 1990, I became more involved. I remember there was an incident with a person called Olodum, who was shot in the hand. MNU decided that I was going to represent us at the press conference. Back then, the women called me "Hamiltinho," and I asked them to call me Hamilton. I went to the press conference. My hands were sweaty, my heartbeat accelerated, and I didn't really know what to say. Without thinking I said, "Our condolences to Olodum." Immediately people were saying, "He's alive, it was a shot in the hand." The people from the left loved to ridicule vulnerable people. This could have prevented me from talking again, but I persisted.

João: So you stayed in MNU from 1990 until when?

Hamilton: Until Rise Up or Die! emerges in 2005. The fact is that when we started to enlist incarcerated people, we reached a lot of people. People in the streets would be saying, "Rise Up or

Die!" Buses were burned. It was out of our hands. That's when the MNU people who were in government cut us loose.

BELO HORIZONTE

João: When did you leave Salvador?

Hamilton: In the late 1980s, I had a son. I didn't have a stable job and I lived and worked inside the MNU in Salvador. Then I had another son, and things became even more difficult. This was when I coordinated and participated in the first SENUN [as mentioned above] and when the MNU folks told me that, given my difficulties, I should go to Belo Horizonte, where there seemed to be more job and organizing opportunities.

I left Salvador on May 11, 1994. I took a bus and arrived in downtown Belo Horizonte, in Praça Sete, where there was an event taking place. I did some poetry there. I liked the city immediately. Food was cheap, there were *restaurantes populares*[8] outside the MNU headquarters where I could have lunch for one Real. Things were looking up. I married, and I had a daughter shortly after. I did a lot of organizing in the city and beyond: I enrolled favelas in the MNU; I was the coordinator for the 1995 March in Brasília[9]; I was the MNU city and state coordinator; and I started the MNU in Juiz de Fora and in several other towns. My aggressive approach worked well with the reflexive manners of the Minas Gerais people—I really loved them. People asked me to calm down, and I asked them to rebel. I participated in all the national Black political events. I did cinema—I appeared in a few films. Because of our work in various favelas, we organized the first national encounter of the Black youth of the favelas. The idea was to have the youth in charge, not adults. Back then, I was in my mid-twenties and I didn't consider myself part of the youth. Today it's different. You have people in their forties who are part of the left youth organizing. And I founded the Teatro Negro e Atitude (Black Theater and Attitude), which still exists.

In Belo Horizonte, I was an articulator of the base [a grass-roots organizer] inside the Black communities. In that city, you have the Avenida do Contorno, which encloses it. The whites live inside of it, while most of the Black people live on the outside. I was always outside the Contorno, and we made a lot of noise. But the Black movement there wasn't very radical—it was contained, cerebral, and wanted to negotiate. I arrived with ire, with anger, and I wanted to fight. So it was natural that I joined the hip-hop folks, the punks, and the transvestites. That is, I joined those who were excluded even by the Black movement. We did a lot of activities together, up and down the favelas.

I was invited to work in Belo Horizonte's Municipal Secretariat of Culture. I asked the MNU leadership if I should accept the invitation. They said that if I accepted the invitation, I had to recuse myself from MNU. I wanted to do the work, and asked to be recused. I started at the Secretariat in 1996. Although some MNU people were against it, most were in favor. I wanted to include people of the favelas in the city's cultural networks. I learned a lot from a great group of people in the city administration: Sônia Augusto, Roquinho, Herzog. I became the administration coordinator while I hadn't even started high school and I didn't have documents. I was about twenty-seven, and I was feeling good. I'd start work at 6 a.m. and came back from all the cultural events at about midnight. I didn't party. It was all work, and I loved it. I felt alive.

João: How long did you stay at the Secretariat?

Hamilton: I stayed until 2001. Two events led to my departure. The first one was the following: Shortly after my arrival in Belo Horizonte, I joined the human rights group Tortura Nunca Mais (Torture Never Again). Dona Helena Greco,[10] who was highly respected by human rights organizations, supported us when everyone else thought we were being needlessly radical and juvenile because, following the MNU, in protest of continued police killings we cried, "Rise up or die!"

After the deaths of three young Black men in a Belo Horizonte neighborhood called Taquaril, we did our own meticulous investigation. It was so well done that, together with Dona Helena Greco, we helped disband a clandestine cell within the Belo Horizonte Civil Police called Igrejinha (Little Church) which routinely tortured civilians. We dug deep into our investigation and began finding out about the Scuderie Detetive Lecoq, a death squad that included José Maria de Paulo, known as Cachimbinho, who wanted to kill Dona Helena Greco.[11] Soon I also became a target.

Around that time, I was arrested because I intervened when police were brutalizing unhoused people. When I told an officer named Vilaça that he couldn't mistreat people, he said, as always, "Who do you think you are, *negão*?" I did just like the Black Panthers and said I could stand at a reasonable distance and, as a citizen, monitor their actions. He then threw me in the police car. A white person came to the scene and said, "You can't take him, he didn't do anything." They took him too. Soon, news crews of TV Alterosa and SBT were there. I shouted, "Call Nilmário Miranda!" who was a representative in congress and a human rights lawyer. Then someone came out of the crowd and said they'd like to be my legal representative. I agreed on the spot. The lawyer came with me to the police station, where MNU activists were already waiting, as were people from the Public Prosecutor's Office.

I was put in jail with the white person. There were only Black brothers, and they were all mad. I said, "Good afternoon, excuse me gentlemen, allow me to go through." They told us to relax and all was cool. But the white person was shaking; he thought he was going to be raped. I played domino with everyone else, and he calmed down. I was determined to defend him; if anyone touched him, we both would be in trouble and probably get stabbed.

I remember leaving the police station with my fists raised, like Mandela. People started to ask me to speak about what happened. I gave talks at hip-hop events, always with lots of people. There were no social media like today, so I had to be there, in person; my body had to be there. That's when they got me. I was at a bus stop [when they kidnapped me]. They took me to a city nearby, in the metropolitan region. They threw me in a bush and put a gun to my head. They pulled the trigger three times, but nothing happened. I ended up walking back home, from Sabará to Belo Horizonte. I was soiled. That was the most traumatic event in my life. I think I still carry the trauma, even though I did therapy and I realized there were many other sequelae. There are sequelae from my childhood also.

It was around this time the second incident happened.

There was a Black kid from the favelas who worked as an intern for us. While doing work at a printing company, he was accused of stealing a cell phone. I went to the kid's house to speak with him and it became clear that he hadn't stolen anything. Later the cell phone was found. Everyone apologized, including the people at the printing company. But I didn't accept the apologies and I wanted to press charges for moral damage. The kid was just a teenager. I asked my secretary Celina Albano to help me press charges. Celina liked me. She was Black and a feminist. But I learned that racism, which for me is nonnegotiable, creates limits. She said she couldn't help me because she couldn't breach the connection with the printing company. I said she would think differently if it was a woman who was unjustly accused. We talked extensively, and the next thing I know she asked that I be fired. I got a thirty-day notice. It was horrible because I had to continue working until my last day. I appealed the decision at the Public Prosecutor's Office, which entered a plea in my favor. But in the end, they fired me.

From that point on, my life went downhill. I separated from my daughter's mother and I was left with my two boys. As they always did, the folks at Geledés sent me some money so that I could leave the city.[12] I ended up staying two weeks, renting a room at a friend's house. Thinking about that political conjuncture, I decided to reach out to James Cavallaro of Human Rights Watch, to see if he could help us in the Taquaril case. He was very nice, and he introduced me to Sandrinha. They helped me considerably.

I stayed for a few more months in Belo Horizonte. I was raising my two sons, one was fourteen years old, the other one seven. Mentally, I wasn't doing well. I was unemployed. Via email, a friend alerted me of a job opening in São Bernardo do Campo, in the greater São Paulo metropolitan region. I did the test and I passed. Candidates were supposed to have a college degree but I didn't have one. I went to work with unhoused boys and girls. The well-known rapper Mano Brown was the honorary president of the initiative. Marquinhos, someone I am still close with, was the coordinator. I did all kinds of things: I was a cook, I was a doorman. It was a difficult time. Some of the unhoused kids were jealous of my own kids. They spat on me. I stayed in a very impoverished and tense favela.

In São Bernardo do Campo, MNU folks were very helpful. I was depressed, I had a lot of internal pain. Every Black person has this deep pain in their chest. I carry this pain. But when you don't have anything, when your children's safety is at risk and you don't know where your next meal is going to come from, this pain gets worse. Honerê, Keto, Rosângela, all Muslim, they were the ones who helped me. With my kids I went to their homes to watch movies; on weekends we cooked together. I went to mosques and I studied Islam when I needed spiritual and emotional support.

So, the MNU was very important. I couldn't be as active as I wanted because I had to take care of my kids. It was a political choice: I was determined to raise my children. I had heard Black women—who were the ones who really educated me—pointing out how Black men abandoned their children. I decided to break that cycle. I ended up not raising my daughter, but I help how I can, and keep in touch. There's a lot of love from my kids' mothers, and I feel good about how things turned out.

It's difficult to talk about all of this, it's like therapy. I suffered a lot: I had no family, I always felt rejected and out of place. I felt I wasn't smart because it took me a long time to learn how to read, to learn math, and it didn't help that, at that time, I hadn't been in college. I had a lot of pain deep in my chest, and that had to do with being Black and in extreme vulnerability. That's why I don't like to be ostentatious. That's why I focus on the most precarious places—prisons, favelas—and I hail people to organize. I do that because I am an example that it is possible to overcome. But it has to be a collective effort, it can't be an individual effort.

In São Bernardo do Campo, too many things happened and I decided to move back to Belo Horizonte with my sons. I was in profound emotional pain, and I couldn't do anything. I then called my *mãe de santo*, and she sang me a song, which is something that is very significant for us in Candomblé.[13] She sang an Ogun song. She said, "Come back to your home." So I did. In September 2003, I returned to Salvador, and in the following two years I got back on my feet. I articulated quilombos in faraway places; the Provocation Wednesdays started.

João: In this loneliness and pain that you felt, in key moments you found people who welcomed and helped you.

Hamilton: I always found those people. Friends, people connected to Candomblé. Any place I go, there will be Candomblé people who will open their doors, have a mat for me to sleep on, and have a plate of food for me to eat. This makes all the difference for someone like me who was unmoored. I found friends with whom I still talk. People from Belo Horizonte, for example. When I became unemployed, there was a time we didn't have enough food at home. My kids still remember how I'd improvise the meals: I'd get bones from the butcher and add them to the beans, and that's what we ate. Sônia and Ablilde would buy three carts of groceries and drop them at my house. There was a lot of affection and love from them. Before leaving for Salvador, they arranged a house for me, and said they'd take care of everything until I was back on my feet again.

When I came back from Belo Horizonte to Salvador, the militant Black youth in Salvador did not know me. You see, the Black movement activist is usually known in the city where they live, and I had been in Belo Horizonte. That's when I started to seek connections and alliances. The first thing I did was get a job and bring back my sons so we'd be together again. I started working with the Black movement in a building downtown, the headquarters of the Associação dos Trabalhadores Rurais (Rural Workers Association). There I met and articulated with various youth movements.

Collaborating with the Black youth, I noticed a new radicality that contrasted sharply with the traditional Black movement where the usual people always talked about health, rights, and culture, and their activities were always in downtown Salvador. We started to move away from those patterns, implementing the concept of communitarian cultural action. I had been part of similar initiatives since the 1970s and 1980s, when I was of the MNU base nuclei. In the communities, I knocked on people's doors asking for food, and we set up a table in the street. Then we talked with people and we conducted theater and/or dance workshops, after which we all ate together. We also had movie screenings in various areas outside the city center. So we already knew what could be done in terms of cultural and political mobilization.

At the same time, vis-a-vis the traditional Black movement, we had a harsher side, which later informed Rise Up or Die!: if a store discriminates someone, we're not negotiating and talking, we break up the store; if someone is called a monkey in an elevator, we confront the person; we're not seeking the police to resolve this kind of thing, we believe in self-defense.

When I got back to Salvador, I also received a lot of solidarity, and lot of help, including from Andreia, my companion in the struggle—she's now in the battle front. Currently, I'm in a different rhythm, not as directly involved. I want to do more literature, I want to do art, I want to write a memoir. I want to cultivate a garden—it would be grandiose to have a community garden. I spent many years going to the Coroner's Office to recognize dead bodies; I buried too many people. Now I want to plant life, plant things that grow and flower. And I'm a good cook, I cook Bahia dishes, Minas Gerais dishes.

GROWING UP BLACK IN PORTO ALEGRE
AND GOING TO MEDICAL SCHOOL

João: Andreia, can you talk about your formative years and how they paved the way for the creation of Rise Up?

Andreia: A lot of what I am and how I see the world has to do with being a dark-skinned Black person in Rio Grande do Sul.[14] I'm not someone who discovered myself Black in college. I was born in a family whose father was Black, my mother is Black, and I have three Black siblings. The conversation about race was always present among us; my parents clearly understood that we had a mark. They always told me, "Because of your Black skin, you will have several negative experiences." I grew up hearing this all the time; the same when I saw my aunts and uncles and other family members. There were no surprises when I left that core family protection. It also made it evident that being Black in a Black space means protection. When you begin to expand your horizons, when you go to school, when you go to the corner store, when you leave your neighborhood where everyone knows you and your family, the mark becomes more accentuated.

I was born in 1972. There's a great impact of the dictatorship in my life as a child. The dictatorship [started in 1964 and] ended formally in the 1980s. I went to a public school. In my family, I'm the third child of four. We're all dark-skinned Black. My mother was a domestic servant, and my father had been a manual laborer until he entered the public service sector. In my school, every Friday we sang the national anthem and hoisted the flag. We had to learn all the national symbols. In 1977, I started preschool. My teacher, Sueli, a light-skinned Black woman, was very affectionate, but there were certain words we couldn't say, like "dictatorship."

My elementary school was named after Dr. Emílio Kemp, a German doctor. It was a great school—it had its own dentist, clinic, and library. Ms. Marley Fernandes was the other teacher who was very important for me. She always encouraged me with praise; she said my hair was nice and that my writing was also very good. She said she was proud of me. She's someone with whom I still talk. I met her when I was eight and she was the calligraphy teacher. Whereas other teachers told me that I could not be the Spring Princess, she told me not to worry about it because I was going to accomplish all the things to which I put my mind. The other teachers were telling me I was inadequate because I wasn't white and blonde, but Ms. Fernandes gave me a positive perspective.

A Black family lived in the school yard. The entire school was a wooden structure, including the house in which they lived. The father and the children were in charge of doing the cleaning outside the school, the mother did the cleaning inside, and an older child did the snacks. There was a staff person, Rita, who was responsible for taking care of the students—to bring them back home, or to stay with them after school if needed.

Until I found Ms. Marley, I used to wet myself. I had a teacher who was harsh and berated me, and called me *mijona*, a local pejorative term. She'd say, "What an ugly thing. The girl is Black and on top of it she pees her pants." This teacher was bad in a heavy kind of way, and Rita protected me when those accidents happened and I didn't have extra clothes. She'd take me home— we lived six blocks away, I knew the way.

Meanwhile my father encouraged us to read, to know the symbols and the history of Brazil. My father had André Rebouças as one of his main intellectual references. Before the name became better known in the last few years, my father spoke often of Rebouças, a Black engineer, lawyer, and abolitionist of the nineteenth century.[15] My father would point out the name of an avenue, "This is Avenida Rebouças," and we'd link the dots between the high concentration of Black people in the neighborhood and the name.

We lived in a neighborhood that had a lot of Black people, and so did my school, although the majority was white given that it was in the state of Rio Grande do Sul. I had many Black schoolmates. I was encouraged to practice sports and I was good at a game called Newcon. I'd often hear, "You have the right physique, you're good at sports." My older brothers also studied at the school, my family was well known, and my father was quite present in the school. He'd say that, "No teacher needs to berate my children. If there is something wrong, there's no need to address my children—they have a mother and a father. You talk to us because we're responsible for them." There were certain things of which we were accused that my father didn't accept. He'd come to school to find out what happened and resolve the issue. We felt protected, we felt that we could talk with our parents without being accused of anything, they cared for us. That was the environment in which I grew up.

In 1982 I went to a school called Champagnat, leaving a neighborhood school for a private school that was much larger. That's when I started to get nicknames, like "Michael Jackson." I had many nicknames, it was brutal. I'd catch the bus and I was constantly scared. I'd often hear, "There goes the monkey to school." It was a type of racial brutality that was new to me. In the Partenon neighborhood I grew up in, we'd go the corner store, it was all very safe. There was a communitarian protection. My father had also grown up there. It's not a wealthy neighborhood, but it had all the urban infrastructure, it had good public transportation. We felt safe in the midst of other Black families. Going to Champagnat, my previous excellent grades got worse. My father eventually understood what was going on. A drawing teacher pointed out that my grades were good in the first two months, and then they fell; he was puzzled. I remember feeling pain in my stomach when I arrived at school. I'd be tense and my hands got sweaty when I had to speak up, because students made fun of me despite the teachers reprimanding them. That's when I started to create my defense mechanisms.

I stayed at Champagnat through middle school. I was part of the school's handball team in the competition that congregated all Marist schools like Champagnat. I did well in several sports, especially in track. There was a white teacher who'd say, "You have a lot of skills, you Black people have a lot of sports skills." Those were the kinds of praise I got, which were also backhand ways of pointing out that I was different. There was a ball for the queen of the school. To select the queen, they put together a group of white girls—Black girls were never included.

Because my older brother and sister also went to the same schools, they, in some ways, opened avenues for me. When I arrived, they were already known as good students. I was a good student too. In 1986, a geography teacher said something I'll never forget: "I know all your family. You may be the only Black family we'll know because we're going through miscegenation." This teacher assigned African literature, she always had Black references in her classes. For example, she talked about Alceu Collares, who was the first Black mayor of Porto Alegre, then the first Black governor of the state. But still, the school had this narrative that Black people's evolution meant integrating with and being diluted by white people, and eventually disappearing. The Black boys' objects of desire were always the white girls.

At home, however, I'd get a different message. Our parents told us they were educating us so that we could have choices. They'd say, "This is a tough world. You're Black people, and the first thing to which people pay attention are your physical traits." They'd stress that we were proud to be Black. They didn't have an academic analysis, but they often talked about their trajectory and linked it to Africa: for example, my father recounted he was raised by grandparents who came from Africa and preserved their history. While we often talked among ourselves, the orientation we got was to not speak much when outside our house.

My extended family was part of the Batuque, an African-Brazilian religion. My father participated in the Batuque circles and knew many of the songs. This had to be very secretive as Batuque was illegal and there was a lot of prejudice against it. So, the introspective and quiet aspects of African culture, which includes family secrets, defined my father—he was always reserved. My father always wore Batuque bead necklaces under his shirt.

My family always had financial difficulties. My father found ways to keep us in school but we were always a year behind the payments. When I finished middle school, my father continued paying for two or three years. He'd say, "Nothing is going to stop you from studying." But it was difficult. For example, I didn't go to the graduation ceremony because we were behind on the payments.

At the end of middle school I took a vocational test. There was a lot of talk around it. Some of my fellow students already knew what they were going to do. They had parents who were lawyers and doctors. We had a neighbor who was a doctor who'd say, "Medicine is always a possibility." On occasions, she provided medical care for us. She told me, "You should do medicine." And, of course, my father always said you can do whatever you choose. When I told him I wanted to do medicine, but that I didn't know how I'd get into medical school, he said, "You will do it," and that he'd help me to prepare.

My brother, who studied System Analysis, had an influence on me. I was uncertain. I did the entrance test for System Analysis. I got in, but I was still in doubt and ended up not following through. Later, I became interested in law. I think that I was afraid of taking the national entrance test for medicine—the high social status of the profession scared me, and we didn't have much of an example. The entrance exam is considered one of the hardest, so I was scared to take it. At one point, my aunts encouraged me to take the exam for an easier undergraduate course. Other family members suggested I finish high school and find a job, forsaking college, which was common at that time. So I enrolled in the Geography college course, which allowed me to be a secretary, and I worked as a secretary for a while.

But I left shortly after; I finally decided to prepare for the medicine entrance exam. Like students today who are eligible for racial quotas—they didn't exist in my time—I had a lot of difficulties filling out the forms, finding the resources to study, and deciding on what specific school to apply for, things that for white people are simple. My parents couldn't help me, and my older siblings were themselves figuring things out. Some of my peers had parents who were professors, who had a ready-made itinerary they could share with their children. But our family's itinerary stopped at the entrance exam. My parents took us to that point, but beyond it there was no reference. So I had difficulty understanding certain things such as the year-long planning. People would plan a year ahead, that was foreign to me. There were exams and colleges all over the country, at their own dates—you had to take the exams at each school—and people would plan their travels accordingly. I didn't even consider schools outside of my state. It took me a while—approximately five years—until I was able to understand the process, prepare properly, and was admitted to a federal public university for medicine.

João: Could you please talk about your preparation?

Andreia: The year leading to my acceptance, I dedicated myself exclusively to the task. I elaborated a plan of study. I continued working, but then I started private lessons for other students who wanted to get into medicine school. When I was twenty-one years old, I became a public servant—I was a clerk in the Civil Police—because I didn't want to depend on my parents anymore. My father was also in the Civil Police; he had been a clerk all his life. My sister and I made the same plans without telling our parents. My father only found out the day we were doing our physical test, and he was against it. He wanted us to go to college. But I got in, and in the next three years I studied for the medicine entrance exam while I worked. I studied by myself. I never had difficulty with any discipline. But I had something that slowed me down: I thought I was incapable. Even having heard my entire life from my parents that I would be able to do whatever I wanted. During those five years, I had that doubt in the back of my mind.

When I got in, I couldn't believe it. I was hesitant. I got in the prestigious Fundação Faculdade Federal de Ciências Médicas de Porto Alegre (the Federal University of Health Sciences of Porto Alegre). I started in 1996 and graduated in 2001. I always felt I didn't belong in that place, among those people. I had no affinity with anyone. No one knew I worked as a civil police officer. At work, I asked to be transferred so that I could have a night shift, and I started working as an ambulance driver. In college, I felt completely out of place. I felt sick, I had gastritis, which is something I had since I was a child when I felt uncomfortable in a new environment. I knew I felt uncomfortable because I was Black.

On the first day of college, it became clear that most newcomers had studied in the city's best schools and they were meeting again at the school of medicine. There's a roll call and I remember the names. The first name was of a famous cardiologist's daughter; the cardiologist had his own research center that specialized in sports medicine. Right after her name is called, the professor says, "I did my residency with your father and we did our post-doctorate together at Johns Hopkins." The professor had comments for the other students too. Then my name was called. I was seventh on the list. "Andreia Beatriz Silva dos Santos." Silence. The professor then welcomed me. The overwhelming majority of students had Polish, German, and Italian surnames. There was the occasional Silva surname [one of the most common in Brazil] but it appeared with a Spanish name that everyone recognized. There were conversations about surnames, and I'd hear things like, "My grandmother came from Poland and we've been here for three generations."

Eventually my presence was naturalized, but it was presence that was silenced. There was a professor with an Italian last name who lectured on the most prevalent diseases. He talked about skin conditions, and said that melanomas were common among Black people. And then he said, "There aren't any Black people here, are there? Ah, I see there is one." Silence. I could tell the other students were embarrassed. He embarrassed me frequently. Yet he was the only professor who mentioned Black people. He went on to say, "Have you ever reflected on why we have almost no Black students in medicine? It's the first time I see one." Silence again. The students who sat in front of me didn't turn around.

Later, that professor came to talk with me. He congratulated me. But throughout my experience in the school of medicine, I was rendered invisible. There was no talk of blackness. I was treated like an exception. Some of the professors couldn't recognize me as a student in that space. That kind of space makes someone like me invisible because it requires that you either assimilate and behave like everyone else—which means you become an accomplice in that system of racial brutality—or you are just silenced and excluded.

One day, a professor in a surgery class mistook me for a janitor and said, "I don't want anyone from cleaning services here, we're about to have surgery; I only want medical students in the room." Before I could answer, one of my colleagues, also a resident doctor, responded, "No professor, she's a sixth-year medical school student." The professor apologized—you know how white people do. But when I protested and said, "Why do you think I can't be here?" the other students disapproved of me: "Why did you have to rub it in? He apologized. You shouldn't disrupt the course's activities." I couldn't help it, I had to speak up.

Almost all the white students were frustrated with me. They'd say, "The professor was mistaken, no one sees you like that. . . ." I often heard, "I don't see you as a Black woman; I see you as medical student." I became closer with the janitors. There's a correlation between dark skin and occupation: the darker one is, the lower one's professional occupation status. The workers at the school wanted to meet me—the one Black medical student. They were my support network.

During my medicine coursework and specialization, most of the cadavers and the patients that I worked on were of Black and mixed (*pardo*) people. At that point, the Universal Health System (Sistema Único de Saúde, SUS) was being formed—the largest in the world. It served all the Brazilian population, the majority of which is Black and mixed.

At home I learned early on that, regardless of where I'd find myself and what I did, I was seen as Black first. We were never to forget that. You carry Africa on your skin. Even when I found myself by a patient's bedside, I'd hear, "I've never seen a resident that looks like you." It means that Africa has no place in such spaces of privilege. I always felt out of place. My body reacted to the antagonism. I was anxious in discussion groups, when presenting at conferences—they were all-white spaces. I had no one I could talk with about these experiences. Two decades after graduating, I still experience similar things here in Salvador. I keep hearing, "I don't see you as a Black woman," or "I've never seen a doctor like you." Black people sometimes say the same things, and they'll add, "You made it."

This was some of my trajectory. I was the only one who worked, and I was always working. I had resistance in my workplace from white people who made it difficult for me to leave early when I needed. But I also had people who supported me on campus. There was a group of upper-middle-class colleagues who made sure that, when we had a test, no one left the classroom until I arrived from work. I wouldn't be able to take the test otherwise. Those people gave me books. They'd buy two and give me one. They were very expensive books, they'd be like one hundred and fifty dollars today. I had a colleague whose parents were federal judges. He'd buy three books, and give one to another struggling colleague and one to me. I had this important network.

But this was also confusing because I knew those people who helped me didn't know what it meant to be Black. They had a perspective in which I was unfortunate and in need, and they were going to help me. They constantly benefited from racism, and I was always the exception. Even though I occasionally found myself in their circles, their reality was so different from mine. I had colleagues who had private drivers take them to school; others spent their vacations in Europe, or in Brazil's northeast, which was very expensive. College was brutal.

I have a white colleague with whom I'm still in touch. She reminded me of when we were doing the obstetrics night shift and a patient didn't want that I cared for her. I don't remember this and other hostile situations. I think I developed survival strategies that include forgetting.

At the same time, I had the experiences in my own family and community. We had cousins who were involved in drug commerce. They had been in prison, and there was a lot of suffering in the family. I had other cousins who became pregnant very early. Also, we often helped family members who needed a place to stay. We had Black neighbors with whom we shared things: we'd go over to get sugar; sometimes we'd go over to lend money. When I was still a kid and my parents had to be away, I'd either stay at a friend's house or someone came over to look after me. We had a network of protection.

College graduation day was very moving. We didn't have money to make a big party like my colleagues did. My brothers helped. We came up with a bit of money. I really didn't want to do anything, but I did it for my parents. We could only invite thirty people. We bought drinks and other things. But my father invited a lot of people and in the end there weren't enough cups for everyone nor was there enough food. He was so happy, and so were the people who had known me since I was a child; they understood the significance of the event. My older brother was the first one to go to college in the entire family, then my sister and me. So it was quite significant. Plus, I became a doctor, which carries with it a certain status.

But in the school's graduation ceremony, on the other hand, I felt I didn't belong. There were eighty-eight graduates and all of us and our immediate families were called on the stage. I got up to receive my diploma with my father and my brother. My mother was embarrassed—she's a very shy person—but when my family walked to the stage, the entire faculty got up. I knew it was to acknowledge the only Black man who was graduating his Black daughter. All faculty congratulated me effusively.

João: Can you please elaborate on your sentiments regarding the offenses directed towards you. The sweaty hands, the stomach ache, how did you deal with them?

Andreia: The first thing I did was to discuss those things at home. My family asked, "What happened, what did you feel?" The dinner table was a moment of reflection and debate. My father would say, "I always told you that it would happen; your mother and I went through similar things. Look at your father, your brother, they're always seen as the exception." He would also ask, "What about your behavior? Do you think you did something that led to people reacting that way?" Sometimes he'd ask those kinds of questions. But more often it would be, "Andreia, we know what that is. You're the only Black person there, and this is bound to happen."

There were a few people in my professional environments who had an understanding of racism, but most of the time it was like, "You're doing well, you're overcoming." At home, though, it was all about the examples of successful Black people. In 1986, Deise Nunes became the first Black woman to win Miss Brazil.[16] She was from my home state. She had accounts of being barred in certain places. But here again, if you're a Black person and you can be integrated—Nunes married a white businessman—you're rendered invisible and there's no more conversation about racism. This happens if you have a certain social status: if you're a doctor, if you graduated from college, or if you're a judge or a senator. Paulo Paim was one of the first Black federal senators, also from the Rio Grande do Sul Workers' Party. He did have a focus on race, but he wasn't radical. We didn't have access to more radical analyses and narratives. There was a Black movement in our state, but it also had people who were light-skinned. In my family, we're all dark-skinned, so a lighter person was considered virtually white. We weren't attracted to that Black movement.

There was party politics, which was very important. Inside the Democratic Labour Party (Partido Democrático Trabalhista, PDT), for example, there were historical groups of Black people, and later the same happened in the Workers' Party. They were quite integrationist. Also, there were cultural groups in Rio Grande do Sul that promoted parties for Black people. We'd go occasionally, but we weren't regulars.

And there were the carnival parties, which were held in private clubs owned by white people. Carnival is very integrationist: although it's a Black event—Black music, dance, choreography—it is owned by whites. So much so that many of the carnival queens had light skin, which in Rio Grande do Sul we called "mulattos." When my mother doesn't want to say a person is not Black, she says the person is a mulatto. At home we'd always talk about these issues. We didn't live separately—in the neighborhoods and in the buses there was no racial separation. Impoverished whites were part of our everyday. Still, no one really thought we were all equal, and there was no mistaking that Black people in certain spaces of privilege were the exception, and therefore hypervisible—all this within the dominant logic of, "We [whites] know you're Black and you're an exception, but we'll treat you as if you were not Black, you worry not."

I was very young when I started to feel in my body the symptoms of the anxiety this logic generated. I had a cardiological evaluation because there was a suspicion I had a heart problem due to my anxiety crises. (The cardiologist also encouraged me to follow medicine.) Since I had symptoms, and also because my grandmother died young from heart problems—she had a heart attack on her birthday in 1970—I did several cardiological tests. In the end, the cardiologist decided not to medicate me, and instead suggested I engage in physical activities and have calming tea when I had an episode. The cardiologist spoke with my mother, and we followed the instructions. But there was no diagnosis, no medication. Physical activity helped alleviate some of the anxiety symptoms.

We've always had a concern about early death. At home we talked about everything, we protected and counseled each other, we hugged and cried together. We figured out behavioral strategies to avoid being so exposed. It was difficult because we were hypervisible and people would inevitably comment on us and our presence.

Years later, in order to better understand my anxiety, I did therapy and sought other kinds of support. I found myself with chronic fatigue and at first I couldn't identify causes. I eventually understood how small aggressions build on each other, and how each apparently small event is in fact profound and meaningful. It's like a very fine needle that touches your heart—you barely notice it, but it will slowly bleed you to death. There are these more homeopathic doses of harm, and there are other events, more like a cannonball, that hit you with sheer brutality.

João: I know these conversations are difficult.

Andreia: Very difficult, but also very important. We confront racism because we are in it as much as the people who are around us. It's important to have a communitarian perspective on it. I think that's why I chose a medical specialty that seeks a communitarian approach to health and disease, which is related to a communitarian approach to fighting racism. For me it's impossible to fight racism alone. I conceptualize myself as part of a collective history. My own family confirms it and acts accordingly. We don't raise ourselves by ourselves; we don't raise our kids by ourselves; and, we can't overcome the daily difficulties by ourselves. Collectively we learn things, including how to take care of ourselves and others. My medical communitarian approach allows an understanding of the ways in which everything that's around us—society, the environment, institutions—impacts an individual's existence. It's an African prism both in terms of analysis and of care.

This collective gaze also rejects individual success, and that's why it never made sense when people told me, "You've made it." And I always think, "Made what? Made it to where?" Is it about having a place to live, to be able to make car payments, eat at restaurants, have access to credit? It's common that people who've "made it" stop right there, and they feel like they don't have to do anything else, including caring for people who are right next to them. For me, to "make it" means not possessing this or that, but to be able to comprehend what it means to belong in a collective and the possibilities that the collective opens up. In this perspective, to be a doctor, even if trained in Western techniques of care, means embracing the collective approach. It's this collective approach that allows me to stay alive.

When we meet someone who is dark-skinned Black, like me, who says that in certain places they feel sick, they don't feel attractive, and that they want to be different, change their hair—that's when we ask that person to look around her, to identify those who helped her get where she's at. That's when you begin to understand yourself, and more importantly, that's when you begin to grasp what can be done together, what we can build collectively, and also what we can adopt as part of our health care. So it's not so much about finding a cure—I don't even know if it's possible—but it's about understanding how one connects with their own self and with the world, and that's how you can find some balance. This balance allows you to say, "I'm experiencing physical and psychological well-being, my soul is aligned and I'm able to stay whole." For me, it is the lack of balance that causes disease.

THE MARK OF BLACKNESS

Andreia: In the process of becoming myself, I had to deal with the mark of blackness. My father and mother helped in many ways. They'd be on the lookout for examples of personal trajectories that helped us. For example, Rio Grande do Sul was one of the first states in Brazil that had a Black governor, Alceu de Deus Collares. Before that, he had been mayor of the state capital, Porto Alegre. My father always mentioned Collares's story: someone who graduated late in life and who followed his own path in the leftist PDT. As a Black man coming from a Black family, Collares was a reference that was very close to our own reality.

My father always reminded us that we were Black, and while we could achieve whatever we set ourselves to do, we had to recognize and deal with the challenges. My parents insisted that we never leave the house without our ID. My father always explained why: "You're Black and when someone approaches you, they need to know that you have a father, a mother, and that you have a family." This was naturalized to such an extent that today I do the same thing. The other day one of my brothers was here in Salvador—he's already forty—and when he went out I reminded him to bring his ID. In our family, we all had our IDs before we could write. If we'd go to the corner store, we needed our ID. The same when we went to school, even if our older brothers accompanied us, and even when our parents were with us. Some people say this has changed, but it has not. I remember recently, when I was out and about with my little brother, someone in a car passed by and said, "Go home you monkey; look at those two little monkeys!"

There's a lot of violence. In the school I went to when I was older there were more white people, and this type of thing happened frequently. At home we'd hear from our parents that, "Unfortunately this is going to continue happening, you have to deal with it in the best way possible—there will come a day when we won't be able to protect you, and there will be a day when we'll be gone." My father always talked about death, it was always present: "When we're no longer around, you'll make sure to always study because that will allow you to have choices."

For me, choosing medicine was related to understanding the ways in which health care can save people. I remember family members getting sick often. For example, my sister and I have the sickle cell trait. Even though the trait doesn't directly cause physical sickness, certain ailments can develop from it. In the 1980s, there was no information about this, especially in Porto Alegre—it wasn't like today, when it has become a better-known topic. I witnessed my aunt getting sick, she lived her entire life under the care of another aunt, my father's sister. She was treated as someone with psychiatric ailments. But there was no conversation about her condition. Ever since her birth, she stayed in a little room where she was taken care of, where she ate and spent most of her time. She did not interact with anyone; she was kept apart from the family.

It was only later that I understood what was going on: how it's related to not having access to formal education, not having choices. How did all of this impact the processes of health and disease? Our predicament made us more reserved; we suffered from added anxiety because there was no available care and diagnostics. Perhaps, this experience contributed to my understanding that in order to improve life conditions for my family and our people more generally, I needed to start with taking care of people's health. But at the time there were no examples of Black doctors; I didn't have the perspective that focused on the health of the Black population (*saúde da população negra*). But I knew we got sick differently and we were treated differently.

I remember that when women in our family sought medical treatment, there was an immediate assumption they were pregnant—even when it was known that they didn't have an active sexual life. But there was always this kind of suspicion, something that didn't happen for the white women in our own community. Similarly, at middle school, when a white student got sad, the teacher would be sympathetic in a way that she wasn't towards me. Even physically I was treated differently. One day, when we rearranged the classroom in a circle, and the teacher said, "Andreia, get that table and that chair." The teacher also said so and so could not lift anything because they were weak, they were fragile. Of course they were white. But to me, the teacher would say, "You can do it, you exercise often, you're an athlete." It's true that I did well in sports, but I never understood why some teachers thought I was stronger than other students. I internalized that expectation and became frustrated when I wasn't able to accomplish a task.

While my acceptance in the school of medicine was an important step, I had to contend with constant and multiple forms of estrangement. The entire experience demonstrated how important my background was—all that had to be in place for me to get there. My grandmother, who left the interior of the state, an area of German colonization; my mother, who was taken out of school and put to work when she was eight years old. At twelve, she started working as a domestic servant for a family in which she took care of a child who was also twelve: she collected the laundry, cleaned the room. While this child went to school, my mother helped with the chores. My mother stayed in that house until she was nineteen, when she married my father.

My father always wrote letters for us. In 1966, six years before I was born, he had been married to my mother for a year and he wrote her a letter in which he said they must lovingly ensure their children didn't have to go through what they had been through. My father started working when he was twelve; he met my mother when he was fourteen. He lost his mother very early in his life, and he went through many incidents of psychological and physical violence. Yet he saw in his family and in the relationship with his wife—who was as Black has he—a path to overcome all the suffering he had experienced. My son read the letter. For me, this letter has become a manual with which to confront the world individually and, above all, collectively.

Here I see a history of people who came before me building possible paths, and I see how my parents continued that trajectory. This reinforces the responsibility I have, not only in personal terms, but also towards my parents and all the people that came before them, and with all the people who look like me. I would not have made it alone. There is no way I could have survived with a modicum of sanity facing so much adversity that in the end is due to me being a Black woman with dark skin, thick lips, a large nose, and curly hair—someone who's not supposed to be in spaces of privilege. I got into medical school already knowing how the world treated me and what it would not allow me to do. The six years of training were very difficult, there were myriad challenges that required constant regrouping on my part. I was treated with unremitting suspicion from doctors, nurses, even the doormen—even though they knew I was a student and had a visible ID on me, they'd ask for another form of documentation to double check. White students never had their IDs checked.

This experience influenced my choice for a specialty within medicine that has a communitarian approach, one that provides the care of family medicine that is attentive to how people live, how they project themselves in the world. It's not a specialty that's concerned with specific equipment and technology, nor with disease; it's a specialty that seeks to understand how people live in the world and, based on their experience, elaborates possible forms of care. It's a specialty that allows me, a Black woman, to exercise my profession taking care of people who look like me. It is based on an approach that recognizes people have a racial identity that's connected to Africa, and how that identity impacts our lives.

PROVOCATION WEDNESDAYS

João: Hamilton, what are the important factors that led to the emergence of Rise Up?

Hamilton: I have what I call a genealogy. Rise Up or Die! doesn't begin in May 2005, as is usually thought. For me, it starts in 1994 with the deaths of Hermógenes and Reinaldo in Rio de Janeiro.[17]

We've always had death as a very close entity. I'm not talking about death as it is understood in African religions, which is good death, a divinity, but death as the interruption of life by the state, which has always been constant for me and for Black people.

Since the 1978 assassination of Robson Silveira da Luz by the military regime's police,[18] the Black movement focused on death as a conceptual debate. But the deaths of MNU activists Hermógenes and Reinaldo shook us up. At that point we realized that our practice had been to report those deaths to legal offices and organizations—state and nongovernmental—some of which had access to the United Nations. Only later we discovered how those people traveled, what hotels they stayed in, what they ate. Those were mostly white people who spoke *for us*, and we were very thankful. And most of the denunciations and demands were about discrimination—someone who couldn't enter a building, who was discriminated against in the workplace, or not hired, things like that.

Still, human rights organizations at that time were not really interested in focusing on racism; they weren't interested in affirming that such deaths occurred precisely because, as Luiza Bairros used to say, we carried the mark of blackness.

The deaths of Hermógenes and Reinaldo, who were investigating and denouncing the actions of death squads and militias involved in drug trafficking, caused no scandal, no national commotion. There were no marches, no rallies, no arsons. Among us, only tears and lamentation. At about the same time, the MNU newspaper on its front page reported a case in the state of Maranhão of a Black man dragged into a hole by a police officer. That article and others stated, "Rise up or you will be killed!" There's also a 1978 poem by Milton Barbosa that says, "Black man, if you don't rise up you will die." From then on, this became a motto for the youth, including me.

In 2004, with Marcos Alessandro and others, we started the Quartas da Provocação (Provocation Wednesdays). It was a mixture of talks, workshops, and debates in which we touched on many controversial themes. For example, we did a series on homosexuality, Além de Preto, Bicha (Not Only Black but Also Gay), inspired by an article in the weekly progressive newspaper *Pasquim*,[19] which ran between 1969–1991 and was critical of the dictatorship. Every Wednesday, we brought together various people to present and debate, and we always had a crowd. Today we have the ongoing series Teoria Sobre Nós (Theory About Us), which is a continuation of the same idea.

The Provocation Wednesdays were a factor that led to Rise Up or Die! From the beginning, we emphasized we were not an organization, we were a campaign against the death of Black people. And we insisted that our collective death amounted to genocide. Black, white, activists, and academics all said that it was a conceptual mistake to call our collective death a genocide because we were part of the Brazilian people. I insisted that we weren't Brazilian, but African, and thus we were in a hostile territory in which we suffered genocide. We supported this claim regardless of the opposition from intellectuals, from people who seemed smarter than us. And when we began to study it, we became more confident. I didn't invent this concept of genocide; it comes from the MNU political formation, I learned it in a classroom, I learned researching and debating it with others, which was a constant aspect of that environment.

During one of the Provocation Wednesdays, we had a discussion on the concept of genocide, and it became central to our way of thinking. In 2005, a United States missioner named Dorothy Stang was assassinated in retaliation for her work with impoverished land workers in the northern state of Pará.[20] Lula's federal government made no effort to find and prosecute the perpetrators. There was a TV news piece whose graphic details I'll never forget. Literally tons of documents from human rights organizations were sent to the government to demand action. We looked at each other and asked: What about all the deaths of Black people that happen routinely and no one notices? Around that time five young people had been killed in the Paripe neighborhood, including the daughter of an MNU activist. They were local petty criminals; they stole, they rode the bus without paying, things like that. Another one had been killed in the Queimados neighborhood. In those areas, small business owners hired off-duty military police officers to kill the youths. So you see, it was the same situation, except that Stang was white, was from the US, and was defending impoverished people—things that made her death scandalous. In response, we wrote a document entitled "All Lives Have the Same Value," and in it we argued that human rights are human rights for white people.

Lourinho, who was a transvestite and with whom I had done theater, was assassinated at about the same time. She was killed not far from where I lived. I went to recognize her body at the Coroner's Office, and saw how they had tortured her. That's when we started a campaign to promote the idea that "All Lives Have the Same Value," against sexism, homophobia, and all forms of discrimination. We crafted a manifesto and organized an assembly at the NGO CEAP (Centre for Pedagogical Studies and Advice). We reached out to everyone, including progressive political parties, religious organizations, labor unions, intellectuals, and artists. Eighteen organizations showed up; Edson Cardoso and Luiza Bairros, longtime Black activists, were also there. This group became a support network. I recall that everyone present had their own story of someone they lost due to lethal violence and police brutality.[21]

In that meeting, we decided to take action—to congregate and protest in front of the State of Bahia Public Security Secretariat. Some people didn't receive it well; they said, "This is craziness, you think you can be like the Black Panthers?" Others said, "We already went through this, it's of no use." But in the end there was strong support, particularly from the youth, so we protested. The Governor was Paulo Souto, an ally of the state's most influential magnate, Antônio Carlos Magalhães, known as ACM, while the Public Security secretary was an army general. There was a strong symbolism in our protest: a bunch of folks from various Black communities confronting a general. We had an all-night vigil and we insisted that no political party and labor union waved their flags during the protest.[22] That was the first source of dissent in our group. Political party people accused us of fascism; others pointed out, negatively, that we were "identitarian" (identitários), essentialists, separatists, you name it. They were basically telling us that we didn't have the correct political analysis, that emotion was driving us. Older activists said pejoratively that all we did was performance, that it was just theater.

This was when Andreia started coming to our meetings. A Black doctor, with a lot of knowledge. She helped us construct an analysis of the police as an institution, how it operated and under what logic. Her presence in our meetings was important, it gave us confidence since we were mostly impoverished and without formal education.

João: All this happened in 2005?

Hamilton: Before the vigil in front of the Public Security Secretariat, in January of 2005 we went to the World Social Forum (WSF) in Porto Alegre, which was a Workers' Party-dominated event, and all the leadership of the Black movement was there. There, two Black youths were beaten up by skinheads. We were upset and protested, stopping traffic; we wanted to end the whole event. We wrote a manifesto demanding a general acknowledgment of the beating. It was entitled "Convene or We Will Break It." The motto was "Sit." We sat on the asphalt. But the people of the Black movement were critical of our action. Still, we brought the WSF to a stop. The event organizers sent several officials to negotiate with us, including the municipal Culture secretary. We told them we'd not leave.

For me, this was the inauguration of a more combative Black movement. I was still part of the MNU at the time, while Rise Up or Die! was consolidating itself in a moment of great political effervescence.[23] We reached the hearts of many young people. It was at the WSF that we scheduled the event in Salvador in front of the Public Security Secretariat. We spent the entire night in front of the Secretariat. Luiza Bairros was there, she spoke at the event, while many other historical Black movement figures didn't want to participate in the act, they didn't feel safe in that kind of protest. But we're militant. Some people threatened to shoot us, to remove us by force, but I think once they saw the great number of people, and so many elderly and children, they gave up. In the morning, the military police showed up to intimidate us. But we held our ground; we blocked traffic—which is when the press arrived and covered the manifestation.

All of this resulted in further dissent within our initial ranks. Especially people affiliated with political parties, they started creating their own organizations modeled after Rise Up or Die! To this day, for example, they protest the deaths of young Black people, often only online. A similar organization was also formed within the governor's own circle with a lot of resources allowing them to cover basic needs for the people in the communities.

We stayed the course. We adopted Black clothing, and we even had a hymn, "To confront the black boots, the black shirts!" (*Pra bater the frente com os bota preta, os camisa preta!*) Since 2005, we've been saying the dead have a voice, and that when we speak, we do so with and for the dead. When we had marches and rallies that weren't well attended, we'd say it only looked that way because the dead weren't being counted. We rendered the dead present.

Andreia: It is important to note that my encounter with Hamilton was prior to the emergence of Rise Up or Die! I show up as a Black woman medical doctor from Rio Grande do Sul. As a Black woman, regardless of what I do, there's a condition that disadvantages us routinely, which means that as soon as I overcome something, something else will take place. So I've always been prepared. My decision to come to Bahia was precisely due to a longing for belonging. I always felt out of place because the majority of the Rio Grande do Sul population is white. Racism there appears subtly as the promotion of integration. To be a doctor in Rio Grande do Sul, I'd have to void myself as a Black person: then I'd be able to navigate all kinds of environments, even when I saw people who looked like me being disrespected and maltreated. In my home state, being a doctor forced me into a situation of racial invisibility.

My encounter with Hamilton was during a workshop organized by young Black people focused on issues of health from the perspective of African history and culture, from the perspective of our place in the world. It was then that I became aware of a militancy that didn't come from established institutions and traditional organizations, the usual so-called activism. From within the MNU, Hamilton proposed that the political discussion be based on the lived experience—it wasn't about formulating an academic thesis on the possibility of our existence, but rather recognizing that the reality of our existence was already imprinted on our skin. In his case, it was about the reality of Curuzu, the neighborhood in Salvador where he grew up, which shaped his experiences and his thoughts.

In the struggle, our mind operates based on where our feet lead us. This approach revives everything that I had heard and learned from my father and from my aunts who'd have to leave their neighborhood at 4 a.m. to arrive at their jobs in downtown at 7 a.m., and would be back at home no earlier than 11 p.m. I begin to see parallels between those experiences and in Hamilton's trajectory—his work in Belo Horizonte as well as in other cities such as São Bernardo do Campo—and how he was able to put all this into a political practice of confrontation.

What does the blood-stained black shirt—which is Rise Up's symbol—mean? What does the manifesto we wrote mean? When we protested in front of the Public Safety Secretariat together with eighteen organizations, what did it mean? It meant we refused to be killed and massacred and we refused to be silent. This was our first step. From then on—and our own internal debates were frequent, intense, and critical—based on my own experience as a medical doctor focused on family practice and community, I gradually came to a more comprehensive understanding of genocide.

At first my participation in debates wasn't very elaborate, but I always understood that when we spoke of the death of Negro

Blul, or when we spoke of the death of Black youth and of police killings, what immediately came to my mind was how all of this impacted entire families.[24] I knew that the mother would never recuperate. Then I remembered my own family's reality: when my siblings and I went out, my mother always insisted, "You can go naked, but you can't go without your ID." To me, it speaks of the slim possibility that you will be identifiable if something happens. It tells of the Black mother's suffering in always and already knowing that they can't protect their child who may be shot in the head, who may disappear. When we started this work, we came across the names of people who had been missing ten, fifteen, twenty years after an encounter with the police. We began to understand the ways in which those mothers entered a state of permanent suffering. The psychology academic debates and literature of the time weren't able to grasp this level of mundane and yet permanent brutality. The mother who had just buried her son killed by the police would see the same police officers back in the neighborhood, still threatening and abusing people. That mother lived in a constant state of terror.

It was at that time that our internal discussions began focusing on genocide. We conceptualized physical death and elimination as a fact with several ramifications that also needed comprehensive analysis. Besides the very graspable element of the physical elimination of a person, there were less obvious effects of a particular death on the family and the entire community. This expanded perspective was a direct result of my constant presence, and the constant presence of Black women, in Rise Up. We had to fine-tune our perspective on genocide. We went beyond the actual number and rates of deaths, which were already catastrophic. Theoretically, we had to consider the various and compounded consequences of each death. In the all-too-common case of a young Black man that's killed, he's not going to have kids, he is finished. His mother is not going to have grandchildren from him; he and his unborn children will not take care of his mother. This dynamic has an impact on us as a people.

From this expanded analysis, we understood the type of care we needed to provide to the families: we'd help with identifying the corpse at the Coroner's Office, we'd help with the burial—often the family could not afford a casket, or flowers, so we'd provide those—we'd offer emotional support, and we'd materially support the family until it was able to get back on its feet. We'd provide basic needs packages (*cesta básica*) to all those who were directly impacted by the death—we'd collect funds, we'd ask for a kilo of rice, a kilo of sugar. We'd also help with the bureaucracy involved in obtaining the death certificate, we'd ask the municipal government about assistance for the victim's family.

The networks of support were formed in that process, in the wake of the deaths that unfortunately never end. We elaborated a specific and far-reaching way of supporting the families, particularly the mothers of those who were assassinated. We understood that we weren't looking at the death of "other people," but rather we knew we could be the next victims; we were all potential targets. We have the same physical traits, we belong to the same people, and that is enough to qualify us as a potential target for various forms of harm and death. While men are the main target, women were profoundly impacted by this pattern of physical elimination.

PRISONS, CARCERALITY, AND COMMUNITARIAN CULTURAL ACTION

Hamilton: Meanwhile, we carried out the work in prisons. It started with letters that I wrote. I'd send the letters via email and those who went to visit folks in the prison would print the letters and pass them on. This was mostly in the Unit 3 (Corpo 3) of the Lemos Brito penitentiary.[25] Eventually, the prisoners invited us to speak with them. When we got there, with Andreia and another activist who's no longer with us, I was already known because my printed letters circulated. We implemented several

long-term programs with the prisoners, including the Circuito
Cultural Intramuros (Cultural Circuit Between Walls), which
included movie screenings, medical assistance, book readings,
cultural centers, and a library. We became strong advocates of
and with the incarcerated people, and the work called the attention of a doctor who worked there, who told us that when we
are here, there's a reduction in mental health medication for
the incarcerated, that folks are calmer, and that they don't fight
each other.

Communitarian cultural action is a central concept for Rise
Up or Die! We've always had culture as a central element of our
political action. To reach people, you can't have a hierarchy about
types of culture, you can't prioritize erudition, or the type of
culture that comes from spaces of privilege like the university or
learning centers. The person who raps, who was or is in jail, is
as important as everyone else.

Of course, this approach didn't just happen. In 2006, when we
met folks from the Malcolm X Movement in the US, they were
also talking about communitarian action, and we added the cultural aspect of it. Our communitarian cultural action programs
have been quite successful. They allowed us entry into many
spaces. We consider every person a bearer of culture and that
everyone is at the same level. We reached places that seemed
unreachable. Many of the folks from the Malcolm X Movement
were related to the Black Panthers. They were very organized.
We took them to the prison, which was very moving because
they had never been in one, and never met any prisoners. They
played soccer with the prisoners, they sang, and many people
cried. They were inspired by our programs and our approach.

When Rise Up or Die! started, it was a novelty. In Salvador,
some Black activists were inside the government, others were
in NGOs, so they were working for those organizations at least
eight hours every day. Our perspective was different. We didn't
have a work day. Our struggle was constant. We'd provoke
people by saying we weren't activists because an activist is one

who comes up with an activity. We were militants because we were in a war. We criticized the typical activists because they stayed mostly downtown, in official buildings, organizing seminars for half a dozen people. Sometimes they had fifty people talking about prisons, but former prisoners and family members were not included. They talked about the death of Black people without talking with family members of those who were killed by the police. Those Black activists were like white people because they liked to talk about Black people, but they didn't like it when Black people spoke for themselves.

When we came together as Rise Up or Die!, we already had a certain courage in common. It had to do with experiencing the military police, experiencing white people in power, and confronting them despite the palpable risks. We protested several times in front of military police stations. We protested in front of Brazil's first police headquarters located here in Salvador. In the early 1800s, this was the base of the military police that destroyed the Urubu quilombo in Pirajá which was led by Zeferina, an African woman.[26] In 1826, the rebellious *quilombolas* shouted, "Long live the Black, kill the white!" They cut the throats of the enslaved Black people who, when given the opportunity to be free, chose to stay with their masters. So we incorporated some of that spirit. When we protest against the police, we shout, "Today you won't kill a single Black person in this town. You thought you destroyed Zeferina, but we came back. You lost!"

In the beginning of Rise Up or Die!, we were criticized for allegedly wanting to revive an aesthetic and a performance of the Black Panthers. We were criticized for being too militant, for not wanting to dialogue with the authorities. We'd say, "We have nothing to negotiate with you. Nothing." What could we ask for? Ask the government to stop killing us? That's what many so-called Black activists still ask for today. We wanted to speak with Black people in their communities and show them that, together, we can fight this gigantic monster. We succeeded. Our first protest was an important landmark because we followed it up with going into the communities. Fearless figures emerged from our ranks. We inspired young people to be outspoken, to be courageous. We created a wave and at one point everyone wanted to be part of Rise Up or Die! Everyone wanted to wear our shirt.

João: What inspired your methods?

Hamilton: Steve Biko's notion of community services was a strong influence, as were the Black Panthers—their breakfast programs resonated with us. That's something we still do. Once a week I'll have a breakfast event with Black men.

We rejected connections with political parties and with elected officials. Because of the rampant corruption in politics, our stance showed our honesty. It was common for politicians to make promises to the communities and, after elected, they never came back. We only spoke the truth. According to our "General Theory of Failure," we affirmed our will to fight and struggle, but we're also alerted that we're not going to succeed, because the state has a massive repression apparatus. Yet we refused to stay quiet. We actually ended up succeeding in many different ways, and we accumulated many lessons in the process.

Our approach was elaborated in the practice, and nothing came easily. We started with community services because that's what we thought we had to do. We cleaned up trash, we planted trees, we cleared backyards, we cooked for unhoused people, and we brought food and cigarettes for people inside the prisons. All of this was important for us. It was from this service approach that we came to the artistic manifestations in those communities. We always worked inside communities seeking to articulate the elders, the youth, and the children. Our cultural action is distinct from the cultural fabrication practiced by middle-class artistic organizations which seek resources and financing. We believe that everyone carries culture, and that culture speaks of the African civilization, which in turn is the only resource we have for our emancipation. We've been active in many different communities, including academia. We've explored local music, poetry, cooking, and that has been a conduit for our communitarian cultural action programs.

We began to bring together the hip-hop and spoken word people. They in turn brought us into their communities, so we didn't have to have authorization to enter those areas because we were with them. We started to organize cultural circuits (*circuitos culturais*), and community film screenings. At that time, between 2005 and 2006, we began to write a *Black Person's Survival Manual in Salvador* on how to deal with a police stop, incarceration, violence, and a series of items that included health and nutrition. That's what we were doing when we came into the prisons in 2006. At that time, we also started conversations about Black masculinity, something that we've been revisiting recently, as you noticed.

The first thing we did in the Lemos Brito penitentiary was to talk with men in Unit 3 because we heard women (who were visiting) had been battered by imprisoned men. The men claimed they were jealous of the women. We showed how difficult it was for women to visit them: it was a long and expensive trip, they had to speak with lawyers, and they had to go through an awfully invasive intimate search. We also spoke with gay men, who during visit days were locked up as if they couldn't be seen by the families. Oppressed people, who were incarcerated, oppressed other people.

The initial conversation involved six hundred men, and if you include their families, there were about one thousand people there. Before the conversation, I spoke with the prison leaders and told them that if the abuse of gay men continued, we'd not return. That conversation became a program. The initial conversation focused on respect for women, and I made a point of stressing that it was I, a man, who was speaking about the vital need to respect women.

Inside the prison we discovered many artists—poets, painters, musicians. We learned that the time we spent with incarcerated people was critical for their mental and physical health.

Shortly after that initial conversation, we met a transvestite, her name was Anita. Until then, other transvestites would hide. There was one who was incarcerated for more than thirty years, and we couldn't find any documentation on her. In fact, she was eligible to get out many years prior, but she begged us not to have her leave the prison. She said, "What will I do outside? I don't have a family, I don't have a job; here I have a job and I have something to eat." Whereas other transvestites were usually humiliated in that prison, Anita got some respect. She became a cook. And since then, when transvestites and gay men say they are with us, they are left alone. Of course we can't protect everyone, but we have a method of moving people between cells and units that guarantee some safety for those who are threatened.

I don't think anyone has this kind of long-term work in Brazil. From Salvador all the way to Ilhéus, Rise Up or Die! was inside the main prisons and we had considerable influence. For example, in 2016 when the state of Bahia government ordered the imprisonment of Indigenous leader Cacique Babau of the Tupinambá people, there was a serious risk that he'd be harassed or even killed.[27] But from Salvador we guaranteed his safety. He had at least eighteen security people inside the prison; he was safe all day and night. A state representative claimed that he was the one responsible for Cacique Babau's safety, but we know it was us.

Andreia: In Rise Up or Die! I found the same Black love that I have in my family. This is why the collective struggle is so important for me. Although they're often celebrated, Black judges, Black doctors, Black teachers, Black professors, and Black engineers do nothing for the struggle. Prior to becoming one of those professionals, I'm a Black woman. Occupying one of those positions does nothing to overcome the pain of racial violence. Only the collective struggle can address it. We have a lot of organizing to do: we need to speak with people from different places who have diverse yet related experiences, from Rio Grande do Sul, Bahia, and Rio de Janeiro to Maranhão. They all know what it is to have their existence as a person denied, they all know what it is to not have a place they can claim their own. They all know what it is to have African markers yet being recognized as neither African nor Brazilian. On the other hand, Brazilians of Italian or German heritage are recognized as Italian or German, even if they've been in Brazil for ten generations. We don't have actual Brazilian citizenship. This is the same for Black people who live in Rio Grande do Sul, where we are a minority, and Black people who live in Bahia, where we are the majority.

Rise Up allowed for people from different backgrounds but with the same experience of antiblack brutality to come together and transform the lives of other people as well as our own lives. It's this transformative drive that allows us to persist in a world that negates our humanity, negates our identity, and our belonging. That's what this collective construction means.

João: Andreia, can you talk about your work in prisons and your take on carcerality as broader phenomenon of surveillance and punishment that includes the entire criminal justice system, residential segregation, punitive schooling, and the healthcare system?

Andreia: There are three factors that compel us to work in prisons. The first is that prisons have a fundamental role in the criminal justice system, the state, and indeed the entire society. It's part of an attempt to not only control certain bodies, but indeed destroy those bodies and minds. It's difficult to measure the full extent of the multifaceted negative impact, but it is an approach that is certainly authorized by society, which in turn benefits from it.

The second factor is the denial of Black people's humanity which demands that we go to spaces where such denial is the

most palpable. In prisons, Black people are not only disproportionately represented, but they're also disproportionally punished
vis-à-vis nonblacks.[28]

The third factor is that we believe everyone's important, and
the prison system provides an opportunity for us to organize and
restructure ourselves as a people. Ever since our first march in
2006, we've had a similar march inside the prisons. We started an
initiative called Cultura e Saúde Intramuros (Culture and Health
Between Walls), in which we apply the concept of communitarian cultural action. Family members are invited to come into
the prisons and participate. In those events, we discuss criminal policies, bias in the criminal justice system, and we also talk
about important Black figures who have been or are incarcerated:
Nelson Mandela, Winnie Mandela, Assata Skakur, Hamilton
Borges. We talk about the ways in which prisons work in other
parts of the world, including the US.

We've been active confronting the state inside and outside
the prisons. We've been discussing the irregular institutional
practices that lead to the greater incarceration of Black people,
and we've been focusing on the unhealthy conditions inside the
prisons. We have documentation showing how the state is the
greatest violator of people's rights inside prisons: from a lack of
water and proper diet, to the complete absence of even a minimal
program that allows for a person to reintegrate into society after
their release. Our premise is that, because we currently don't
have the power to destroy prisons, we strengthen the people who
are inside as much as we can. We try to provide elements with
which they can begin to restructure their lives while incarcerated, and we also encourage that they become politically active
and consider collectively opposing a system that works against
our existence.

It's been seventeen years doing this work inside the prisons.
We're trying to assist people while they're incarcerated, but also
reconnect them with the outside world, and in the process we
restructure families. Women, in particular, have far greater diffi-

culties in restructuring their lives and not coming back to prison. Most Black women are domestic workers. It's difficult for them to resume their occupations once they're released. They often have children and other people who depended on them. When a Black woman is incarcerated, her family is shattered and her children are separated. When released, she has the extra burden of trying to reconstitute her family. It's not uncommon that their previous male partners have left them and constituted another family; sometimes they're also incarcerated, or dead.

When we try to address these and other issues related to the dehumanization of prisoners, we encounter considerable resistance from the prison staff and administrators, so we're constantly trying to find ways around the system. Inside the prisons, we promote debates against prisons, against incarceration, and against the prison policies. Our critique of course creates strong resistance against our presence in those spaces. It's hard work to be carried out autonomously.

Our goal is to construct institutions that welcome and aid formerly incarcerated people and their families by providing legal assistance, job training, and actual jobs. We want to provide networks that bring together the formerly incarcerated and those who did not have the experience of being caged. We think that people can learn from each other how to avoid imprisonment, and also how to organize and rebuild their communities.

It's hard work and we need to be constantly very attentive. There are many traps, especially cooptation. We have to remind ourselves that the system is against us and will use whatever means necessary to stop us. There are people who are now in the state machine, or in political parties, and sometimes they are used against us. A number of our former members join the ranks of the state, and they try to coopt us. For example, they plan a musical show inside the prison, believing that it will be beneficial for the prisoners. But they don't take into account that, when we have cultural events inside the prisons, we also have discussions on politics, health, sexuality; we bring food and hygiene items like toilet paper, toothpaste, tampons. Of course they're not thinking along those lines.

João: As a medical doctor who works at a prison, how do you deal with this constant negation of Black people's humanity?

Andreia: Let me reflect on this via *The Underground Railroad*, a novel by Colson Whitehead. I saw the series before I read the novel. What strikes me is how people survived the extreme conditions of slavery, and how those who were free led their lives knowing that most people remained in those conditions. I want to draw parallels with our current time. How can we celebrate anything in this country when we know that a great number of people live in conditions analogous to slavery? I bring this up because, as a people, at times we seem to have the conditions to confront the state. At other times, we don't. I go back and forth on this. The processes that affect Black people—incarceration, varied forms of societal exclusion, early death by preventable causes, which are part of a cycle of imposed vulnerability—are not included in the white political agenda. That's why we in Rise Up emphasize the need for the project to be Black-centered.

In a context in which the state neglects and kills us, we found that culture opens doors: people's experiences, histories, memories, songs, and rituals can't be taken away, even if they exist only in our heads. That's why we chose it as one of our main tools; it can reconnect people with their communities, with their humanity. We bring creative people inside the prisons to talk about poetry, music, dance. It has helped people talk about their trajectories and reconnect with themselves and their communities. In the events we organize, many imprisoned people share songs they know, write and recite poems, and remember specific family recipes and teas for various ailments, including parasites.

Our own editing house comes from this realization—that we need to reconnect by telling our own stories and focusing on our own experiences. We began to have book launching events inside the prisons, and we invited several authors to give talks and participate. We had children's books, fiction, biographies. And people would read them, even those who were just beginning to learn how to read. We stimulated reading circles in such a way that who could read would read to those who couldn't. It was common to have a cell with twelve people in which only one or two knew how to read. People read poetry to their cell mates.

In that context, one of the most important things we did to reconnect people to their own existence, and to that of their families and communities, was to have an open mic invitation for people to share a childhood memory—it could be anything: a dish, a game, a song, a poem. That's when we discovered that many of the incarcerated people played instruments, knew about medicinal herbs, and had an array of songs and poems committed to memory.

We've done similar events outside the prisons. We've had events on care. I learned from some of my professors that the medical consultation is an encounter between two technicians. One of them is a trained technician of care who learns about the human body and a bit about the human mind, about behavior, physiology, disease; the other person knows about themselves more intimately than anyone, which in itself is a technique. From that premise, I understood how much could be done in such a space of deprivation. First, I had to recognize that, with the person in front of me, from individual and collective perspectives, we could combine our knowledge and promote something that's more than the absence of disease. We can promote something that can transcend the body and includes not only access to resources, but also possibilities of being. There's a holistic health concept established by the World Health Organization that includes bio-psycho-social well-being. But when we think of a Black person in the world, that is not enough to establish what health should be. In Brazil we also have a broad concept of health that attempts to conceptualize the person in an integral way that includes access to land, work, income, education, freedom, and health itself.

But for those of us who are Black, our humanity is denied. The WHO and the Brazilian health concepts build on a notion of the human and humanity, but those don't apply to us. Dark-skinned people inside prisons, for example, have their lives negated as a matter of routine. So our notion of health needs to be elaborated, or re-elaborated, from this recognition that Black people are not seen as human. We need to rebuild the very concept of humanity and then we can reflect on how to promote health. In the medical consultation, when there's a mutual recognition, there's a reconstruction of humanity—both mine and of the person who's seeking medical care. Based on this encounter we can then build a more relevant notion of health.

This process is unique to each person who seeks care. Each person is attempting to find a small piece of their own shattered humanity—it's not a linear process. But it's a search for which, once we reconstruct what health means, we can provide what the person is in search of and make them feel better.

After seventeen years as a family and community doctor in those kinds of spaces, I see myself being affirmed and affirming others in dialogue. When I ask people what they think we can build in terms of health, people always go back to a before, an anterior moment, a previous pain, an immeasurable pain. In those moments, it's possible to revisit and reflect collectively. So when I entered the space of the prison, I had the confidence I could contribute. It doesn't mean I can guarantee health to others, but I think that it's possible to promote this process of dialogue between people who have the common experience of having their humanity negated, and from it reconstruct what health care and well-being mean.

Thus, it's impossible to approach a person with an ailment that manifests itself physically without taking into account racial brutality. I can't assume this person had a different experience from mine. I need to find ways to care for this person and transform their life, be in the space of the prison, the street where I live, or in the struggle we carry on as a political organization.[29]

GROUNDING IN BLACK COMMUNITIES

Hamilton: When Rise Up or Die! emerged, we changed how to politicize the death of Black people. Because up until then, we only counted our dead, we only lamented and cried, like people still do today. So we asked, what can we do? We decided to go to the communities, and ask them what should be done. One of the things I learned in São Bernardo do Campo was to address masculinity. Sérgio Barbosa, a Black medical doctor, introduced me to the work of anthropologist Osmundo Pinho. Up until then, I knew Pinho from capoeira that we both practiced—I had no idea he was an academic. That led me to discuss masculinity in our work in prisons. So while there were theories on masculinity, I made the topic a concrete exercise. We prepared the food ourselves, and as we ate we had conversations with imprisoned men about sex, sexuality, work, grief. When we did the events outside the prisons, the men would cook and then invite the women to share the food and talk with them. Soon, we had organized caravans into the communities. DJ Branco, who did this with us, had a very good video camera with which we captured several complaints of abuse, torture, assassination. We then started to systematize this information and crafted what we called a "Rise Up dossier." We gathered all assassination cases and sent it to Clare Roberts, who was a Special Rapporteur on the Rights of People of African Descent and Against Racial Discrimination in the Inter-American Commission on Human Rights.[30]

I was angry, and I was feeling what we call creative hatred. We created our own look. We dressed in black. We created our own language because we had dialogues with a wide spectrum of people, from well-known criminals to respected judges, artists, and intellectuals. Young people were attracted to and joined us, and this created a rich and dynamic cultural atmosphere. We continued with the communitarian cultural action, which was always fundamental to us. We went to different communities reciting poetry, we reached out to the musicians to sing and play with us, we asked the elders to tell their stories. We also had a cinema club.

Our work in prisons drew from all those initiatives. We expanded our work in the prisons in such a way that all units were connected to us, and we achieved the feat of being respected inside. We never accepted bribes, we never accepted favors. We knew their money came from crime, we knew it came from the same place as oppression. We were scrutinized by the police and often investigated, we had our phones tapped, but they had nothing on us.

I found my own way of being an activist when MNU expelled us. By then, MNU didn't have a community experience; it was mostly an instructional, party-influenced, and government-focused formation. We didn't fit there. We created our own space through our practice. We developed a series of concepts that many people later adopted. We came up with the General Theory of Failure,[31] which posits that when the police arrive to kill us, we're practically dead already. We decided to be serious, not smile. We began saying, "Our dead have a voice." We said it in 2005 when we started, and we continue to say it. We worked nonstop. Often the phone rang at 3 a.m., and off we were, dealing with some emergency.

The people who join Rise Up are those who have lost relatives, who have been brutalized, people who live in racially separated communities. That's a concept we developed. Those are communities in which the state only enters to kill people.

On the other hand, the people of the Black movement, for the most part, don't want conflict. Those people don't want to collaborate with us. In episodes of mass killings by the police, they don't show up. At best, they protest online.

We're not done, and we want to do things differently. We want to reinvent ourselves. I'm almost sixty years old. Rise Up needs to make space for children and young people. Our members Nélio and Silvana are currently twenty-four years old. Many started with us when they were kids, teenagers. They were struggling with us. We were in such a maelstrom, in such a hurry, that we didn't even know their age, but they were there.

João: Can you please talk about the various Black diasporic influences that you frequently mention—Winnie Mandela, Steve Biko, the Black Panthers, Amílcar Cabral, Assata Shakur, among others—how did you come across them? I'm thinking of the difficulties in translating and in getting a hold of books. How did you get familiarized with this diasporic Black radical tradition?

Hamilton: Since the 1980s, the MNU's formation courses have been the source of that information. In the formation courses, those who were older than us shared much of what they already knew. Today, those courses don't exist anymore. People are now thinking about diplomas and certificates to grow their personal curriculum. There's no more knowledge for the sake of knowledge, or art for the sake of art. There's always some ulterior personal motive. Now, if your knowledge and your art can serve for liberation, it's even better, and that's what we're after.

Salvador always had a lot of Black radicals coming and going from all over the world. In the 1980s, because of the dictatorship, we couldn't be too open about this, but there was a lot of underground intellectual activity. Inside the MNU we had a lot of theoretical discussions, and we had to be very well rounded, we had to read and debate constantly. The elders taught me to wake up early to study, to read; and I also learned that writing is a way to ease your mind. I remember someone telling me that "Who writes endures" (*Quem escreve permanece*), and I started to write early on. I liked to write, even though my writing then was not good.

I always read extensively—even when I didn't know how to read that well. One of my first encounters with Malcolm X was via a US woman who read and translated for me—she told me I had to know all about him. Winnie Mandela's *Part of My Soul* guided us. We also reproduced, quite literally, Steve Biko's thoughts in a lot of what we said and did. We participated actively in the campaign for signatures to free Nelson Mandela, and that put us in contact with many people in Brazil and abroad, which in turn generated more suggestions for readings and resources.

João: Could you talk about the MNU formation courses and/or other aspects of your trajectory that contributed to your political perspective? Taking into account what you said earlier about "nothing falling from the sky," regarding your insights and your approach to politics, including how you perform your ideas in public—which is always compelling. Can you elaborate on key influences?

Hamilton: One of my earlier memories is of the Blocos Afro (Afro Blocs), which had composers who were very respected and became our idols. We wanted to be like them—they were handsome, they were public figures, and embraced by our community. To be a composer, you had to study and do research. You had to know the history of Africa, you had to go to the library and local organizations who had resources. There was a composer called Boboco, whom I wanted to honor, he has a song that I always remember, "O meu povo irmanado avança o universo, no canto eficaz que ultrapassa a barreira do sol, e quanto ecoado esse canto faz ebolição criado pelo poderio de um povo Ashante sagrado e tão fidelíssimo no centro sul em Confederação comandada por Osei Tutu ile ayie faz nascer nas matérias amor pela vida."[32] This person looked like me, he was a bit older than me, and he was my inspiration. That's one of the reasons I sought information, I read, I went to the library and I learned how to make notes. It was because of the Ilê Aiyê carnival bloc. My first foray into the history of Africa happened because of that bloc.

When I joined the MNU, I was intimidated and shy, as I'm still today. There were many people who were in college, who had sophisticated vocabulary and analysis, whereas I was from the ghetto (*maloca*). I was afraid to speak up, which in retrospect was an error.

The MNU formation courses were difficult. They were on Saturday at 9 a.m. If you wanted to do well, you couldn't party on Friday. You had to be disciplined. There was a sense of being watched and taken care of. The older militants would reprimand those they saw drinking. I remember one instructor for the Political Formation class. He was about my age. Very serious, and at the time he was an undergraduate in history. There was an emphasis on Marxism, and there were several currents in the movement, including Leninists and Trotskyites.

We also learned about "Tática 2," which was how the police and even competing groups infiltrated organizations and used intimate relationships to extract information, plant dissent, and fabricate rumors and do harm. In Rise Up we're very careful about this, and we alert all our members to be careful about who they relate with and date. When someone shows up and begins dating one of our activists, it can be a trap to expose our group by linking the Rise Up activist to drugs, violence, and sexual abuse.

MNU members often cleaned our own headquarters. We provided services to the community: we took trash out, weeded overgrown areas, and we organized plays and open cinema sessions. I've always been a base activist, and this helped considerably in how we formed Rise Up. We had a course and several encounters on Pan-Africanism. The formation I got in MNU helped me to participate in debates with the president, the governor, and police officials. I don't fear anyone intellectually. We've debated with academics from various parts of world, and when we disagree, we hold our intellectual ground.

João: Could you compare the MNU formation courses with the Black men circles Rise Up organizes today? If I'm understanding correctly, the Saturday MNU courses were part of a sequence. What are the similarities and differences between them?

Hamilton: Yes, MNU courses were part of a sequence, and they were varied. There were courses to form electricians, boxing classes, history of Africa. There were heated debates for which we prepared extensively: each of us wrote essays and then we'd defend our ideas publicly. We had debates about literature. There were activities on Saturdays and Sundays, you hardly had time to rest. There were meetings all the time.

In terms of similarities Rise Up, like MNU, emphasizes discussions on gender and sexuality. The difference is that in MNU women were the ones debating gender—I was always around them and participated in many of those debates and study groups. There was a Group of Women inside MNU. Men were not very keen on participating. Today we're conducting a similar debate, with honesty, and we're seeking transformation. Rise Up has groups of men discussing gender and sexuality, which was unimaginable in MNU.

Another similarity is the fact that, alongside the debates, the study, the preparation, and all the hard work, in the MNU we also made time for relaxation and hanging out.

It was difficult for MNU to attract people into their ranks—there was widespread resistance against the discussion on race, especially during the dictatorship, which monitored MNU, infiltrated it, and considered it subversive.

Today, the difficulty is that Rise Up is often seen as masculinist, and that prevents some people from coming to us. A transgender person who was in Rise Up had the same initial impression. This person transitioned while in Rise Up, and initially she was part of the men's circle. At one point, she decided to dress like a woman, and some people tried to ridicule her. We supported her and guaranteed her protection, and told her she should do as she pleased regarding her gender. She told us that Rise Up allowed her to transition. I credit the men's circle to that success. Her transition was a victory for us. Sometimes we think none of what we do is important, but in this case one person's life was transformed. In those circles we see many people suffering, going through trauma, and the circle provides a space of reflection and support. She later said that we weren't masculinist, but we were hard on people. That is true. Our narrative is confrontational, and we don't mince our words.

Women in Rise Up are taking over the more important aspects of the organization. I'm stepping aside, and concentrating on organizing and facilitating the artistic events and the intellectual debates, including the men's circle. We plan to have regular events, at least one per month. I also want to travel more, and create men's circles in various locations.

I feel very tired, and a bit unwell. That's why I want to concentrate on activism that won't bring trauma, like dealing with dead and disfigured bodies, incarcerated people. I'm done with that, it's been too much.

João: Andreia, 2004 is when your contact with the group of people that becomes Rise Up or Die! takes place. Can you please talk about how you ended up in Salvador?

Andreia: My decision to come to Bahia [the state has the greatest proportion of Black people in the country] results from this search for belonging, from a yearning for being among people who look like me. I wanted to build something that was greater than just a personal project.

I had come to Salvador for the first time in 2000, for a conference. I came with my parents. I felt I belonged, I felt at home. I could see myself in the streets, in the stores, in the hotels, among the workers. I remember telling my parents, "I'm going to come back because here I'm part of a majority, I'm not a minority like in Porto Alegre," where I was born and grew up, where my family and I were constantly rendered invisible. In Salvador, I don't need to justify anything. This feeling was immediate. When I reflect on how I got to Salvador, I immediately remember how I was mistreated in Porto Alegre. I told my father, "I have to come back," and he said, "Yes, if you identify with a place, you have to come back."

In 2002, there was a national selection process for medical doctors who wanted to be based in small cities, less than twenty thousand people, and that had a low Human Development Index. I ended up in Ribeira do Amparo, a small city of fourteen thousand in the interior of the state of Bahia. I arrived with white health professionals. It was the usual story: people would address the nurse, who was white, as if she were the doctor and she'd say, "I'm not the doctor, the doctor is Dr. Andreia." People would say they'd never seen a Black doctor.

On weekends, I'd come to Salvador to check out the political scene, and figure out how I could contribute. I began having more contact with people involved in the Black movement. In 2004, Rita Santa Rita, who was part of a Black women's group in Alto da Pombas, a central neighborhood with a long history of activism, invited me to give a talk on Black people's health. This was perhaps for the holiday on October 12. I didn't hesitate. Even though I wasn't much aware of it, there was already a strong debate about the health of the Black population, a debate about equity within SUS (Sistema Unico de Saúde—the national Universal Health System).

From then on, I began having a better understanding of the issues within the debate. I remember that while doing my medical residency in Porto Alegre, in 2001 and 2002, I tried to conduct research about cancer screening on Black women in the city. There was no data on it. In Bahia this discussion was more advanced, and there were groups of people, especially Black women, already discussing these types of issues. This indicated to me that I needed to continue to be in dialogue with those groups and forge a way forward, even though the path was not yet clear. In Ribeira do Amparo, the small city where I was based, I organized discussions about those topics. Although many Black women there understood that the medical treatment they received was not equal to that of other women, there was no vocabulary to articulate their perception.

I met Hamilton in 2004, at a meeting in Salvador about confronting racism. By then he had a long trajectory of activism with far greater racial consciousness and a greater familiarity with the relevant debates. He talked about the history of Africa; he had this very close relationship with young people, who recognized themselves in him and in the things he was saying. His approach was captivating, and in the meeting we ended up using some of it in our activities. For example, to incite debate, we played a song by [the hip-hop group] O Rappa, which Hamilton had cited. We used a part of their song which said, "Peace without a voice is not peace, it's fear." We used it to talk about what kind of peace we had, what it meant for us. We suggested it was the peace of the cemeteries, it's the peace of dead people who cannot talk, and we need to hear those voices.

That's when I became more knowledgeable about the history of Black activism in Bahia, and the racial debates in Brazil. This confluence of people and ideas put me on a path from which there was no going back. And I think this is also related to all that my family put in place. To imagine that my grandmother died of a heart attack in 1970, when she was only fifty years old—when life expectancy for the general population was sixty years. She was a dark-skinned Black woman. She and I are physically alike. She lived in a German-colonized area where she had to teach her children a German dialect so that they could work as domestic servants in the homes of those people who claimed German ancestry. This was more than two hundred kilometers from Porto Alegre, the state capital. And then, in search for better conditions for her family, she migrated to the capital. She worked as a domestic cleaner. In terms of vulnerability to racial brutality, she lived in extreme situations. This is still very present in me.

I thought it was strange that in Bahia I hardly came across other Black doctors, and I was in the city with the greatest pro-

portion of Black people in Brazil—the city with the greatest concentration of Black people outside of Africa. To me it was weird
that I, who was still relatively inexperienced, was the one called
to talk about Black people's health.

All this was in the end of 2004, and from then on, I got closer
to Hamilton and our history becomes entangled with that of Rise
Up or Die! From then on, we were building things together.
Given the issues of life and death of Black people on which we
focused, my practice as a doctor was important. In January 2005,
I was assigned to be the Health Coordinator at another small
town called Maragogipe, where I started having closer proximity
with the quilombo people and their health problems.[33] At that
time, there was no national policy on Black people's health, but
we were already discussing it. We focused on the ways in which
racism determined how doctors and medical institutions treated
Black people. It was a difficult conversation because there were
conflicting views on blackness, and there were doubts about who
was in fact Black. In the field of health, it was just as difficult. Still,
our nascent debate on health and race—one that was in many
ways pioneering—provided me with a solid base from which
to develop my practice as a doctor. In Rise Up, we emphasized
that racism determined the kinds of treatment people received.
Why didn't the quilombo people receive adequate treatment?
Why were health care facilities historically concentrated in central areas of the city? Why was there such a restricted menu of
treatments offered?

I participated, even if timidly, in the discussions and debates
that led to the May 12, 2005 vigil [from which Rise Up was for-
malized]. I organized a group of medical professionals; I raised
funds for coffee and food; we brought people from the interior
of the state to participate in the discussions during the vigil.
It became increasingly evident to me how important it was to
have an autonomous and independent organization, and this
would allow for a more informed and robust approach not only
to Black people's health but also more broadly to Black people's

well-being. To me, there was an emerging understanding that it wasn't just about treating disease or promoting healthy practices; it was about life itself. Consider a Black woman who had lost a son, or who was still looking for a son after his disappearance fifteen years earlier; in terms of health, what were her needs, and how could we provide for them? What's the approach that's possible? That's when I began to have a better understanding of the issues.

João: Could you talk about what experiences prepared you for the formation of Rise Up in 2005? Specifically, how did the MNU influence Rise Up's guiding principles? It seems to me that, while there are obvious continuities between MNU and Rise Up, there are also obvious departures.

Andreia: I have never been affiliated with other organizations. Given MNU's relevance in the history of Black struggle in Brazil, we're respectful. I always try to be careful when talking about MNU, because we are not in opposition to them. We surely drank from that fountain. I know of the MNU through Hamilton: what he experienced and the vast materials he has collected about them, including dissertations, newspapers, essays, photographs. He played an important role in the organization, and was in it for a long time, so in my view we're not in opposition to them, although we have critiques.

Hamilton: Regarding our work in the prisons, in the beginning, incarcerated people painted murals with "Movimento Negro Unificado" in them, and we helped to get more than 300 people affiliated to MNU. In the beginning, we were a marginal group within MNU, carrying out a political perspective that was contrary to what MNU wanted. I'm from a historically Black community in Salvador; I had an earlier participation in labor organizing. So, when I became a MNU militant, they respected me. We gave MNU considerable visibility because we did work in communities to which no one had access—and that is not an exaggeration. We worked in the most impoverished, the most destitute and violent communities. The opposition from MNU folks became more evident when elections happened because we became increasingly critical of electoral politics.

Back then I worked for a state representative in the national congress. Like everyone else in the MNU, I believed the parliament could be a space to strengthen the Black movement. But people ended up doing the work of the movement inside the parliament. That's when my take on this became more radical. If you look at the beginning of Rise Up or Die!, if you look at the photographs, you won't see any labor union or party flags. For most people in the Black movement that were inside political parties, our stance was despicable. We opposed the Workers' Party's white Jewish candidate, who was actually from Rio de Janeiro, for governor of Black Bahia.[34] From that point on, we insisted on distancing ourselves from political parties. But our influence on the debates within the Workers' Party and other left formations remained. For example, there was a discussion about human rights and public security. In Rise Up, we'd say that we're not for human rights because those rights are for whites. "We're not part of human rights, we're a Black social movement." We wrote a manifesto about it. At that time, in the neighborhood of Canabrava, five young people had been murdered by the police, three of which in front of their mother. This was symbolic of what we were dealing with; we're all affected by events like that.[35] I was upset for a long time and needed time off to recuperate.

In the meantime, there was a meeting to discuss public security in which several state and national representatives, and an MNU city council member, were present. I vehemently opposed their views, which of course irritated them. Also, we got a lot of imprisoned people affiliated with the MNU. That was the last straw, and led to my calling for an ethics commission at MNU. According to the elders, I was endangering the entire organization because I was linking it to incarcerated people, to organized crime. We thought MNU would sue and claim our name because "Rise Up or Die!" actually comes from their trajectory. But it's very difficult to sue us. You know why? Because we have nothing to lose. We don't negotiate, we don't bargain. Our formation, from the beginning, has been one of opposition. We're a ragtag group of people who are persecuted, destitute. From the beginning, we've been beaten to the ground; there's nowhere lower for us to go. So they never sued us.

We continue to show respect for MNU, but we have to say it: their political agenda is a party agenda. Our agenda tells the people that they can have their own schools, they can do things autonomously as they find best. Luiza Bairros used to say that, "The social movement took to the streets to lose." We in Rise Up separated from MNU and political parties to lose—in a way we've already lost, you see? When we present the terrible numbers on public security from the Lula government, and how particularly Black people were affected, who wants to listen to us? Even in the communities, where a lot of people are psychologically ruined with drugs and alcohol, they don't believe we can get together on our own terms and begin to turn things around. So today we're back to the moment when Rise Up emerged: we deal with reality, with our feet on the ground, we weren't born to promise salvation. Our head is where our feet are.

João: Andreia, you described the ways in which, around 2004, the debates about the Black population health were emerging and began resonating with you. What were the specific questions in that debate that were relevant to you? Also, related to your parents' experiences, where do you think their consciousness comes from? You mentioned domestic labor early in their lives. You also mentioned the consciousness of racial brutality, and how the letter that your father wrote in 1966 becomes a reference manual. Much of what you shared sounds like a series of traumas you and your family and your community experience as a fact of life, as a daily event. I imagine your daily medical practice is also full of such events. For example, there's a diasporic fact that a great number, if not most, of the cadavers medical students work on are Black. Lastly, you mentioned having the sickle cell trait, which made me think of how the Black Panthers developed a sickle cell screening program.

Andreia: I'd like to address all of these points, I think they're important. I'd like to start with my parents' history and why I value that letter. Because of my father, we grew up listening to samba—he asked us to pay attention to the lyrics. I grew up listening to Luciene Rodriguez, a samba musician. Samba expresses some of our history, the history that my father associated to that of Black people. On Sundays, during our regular family gatherings, we'd barbecue, which is typical of Rio Grande do Sul, and listen to samba. My father referenced the lyrics when speaking with us. He developed this family practice because he lost his mother when he was very young. He was raised by an uncle who was quite aggressive and violent toward my father—today it would be unacceptable. My father had scars on his back; he'd hide them but later we found out they were from his uncle's beatings. My father didn't talk much about this. He started working at the age of twelve. He worked from Monday to Saturday, he had very little down time. Whereas my grandfather was a longshoreman, my father worked packing up coffee. My father wanted to find someone who had the same wish to start a family. He gave all his earnings to his uncle, who gave him a bit in return. One day, when he went to the market to get the coffee, he walked past my mother, and they looked at each other. He found out where she worked and asked her bosses if he could visit her. They told him he'd have to speak with her mother, which he did.

When my father met my mother, he was embraced by my grandmother, who took him as her own child. After a few years of dating, he started living with them—they had a very good relation. He was alerted that it was best if my mother stopped working for the family that employed her because it was known they had a pattern of abuse towards the women domestic workers. Soon, he said he was ready to contribute to the household. My mother started preparing for the wedding. The wedding ritual was particularly important for my father because he considered it the beginning of constructing a path of happiness and of possibility. In 1966, a year into the marriage, he wrote the letter in which he states that love intensifies in the building of possibilities together. He affirms that he doesn't want anyone in his family go through what him and my mother and others before them went through.

My mother comes from a lot deprivation at the same time in which, in her circles, women had the role of taking care of others and push out men when necessary. My grandmother had her first marriage in the 1950s, and then separated from a man who was violent. As you can imagine, separated women weren't well regarded, especially a Black woman in Candelária, a small interior town in the state of Rio Grande do Sul. My family suffered from stigma because of that. The decision to leave for the state capital, Porto Alegre, was partially due to that stigma. I think the encounter between my parents had to do with both of them wanting to have a family. They were both very caring and strong at the same time. They were both very communicative with us, would often talk and show things. For example, there was a free health clinic, the Santa Casa de Misericórdia, and when we'd pass by my father would remark that the people waiting in line were unemployed and that's the reason they didn't have access to health care. He'd stress that we needed to plan ahead to guarantee health care by securing employment. That's how we grew up, with my father showing real life examples. He had a lot of old sayings, like, "You can't whistle in the house at night," and we'd obey and repeat them, even if they didn't make much sense at the time, because we fully believed in what he said.

In our house, my mother was responsible for the food, that was her job. Each one of us had our specific functions. I often heard the following: if you eat everything now, your brother won't eat; if you eat everything at mid-day, there won't be any dinner. Both my parents told us how much each item cost, and reminded us that if we wasted anything, we'd be responsible for all of us not having food. I had the understanding that I could not eat all I wanted. Also, my parents would instruct us on how to shop. My siblings and I would be responsible for the money and my parents would say, "You have this many Cruzeiros [the Brazilian currency at the time] and you can buy this specific amount of meat. A kilogram of meat costs this much." And they'd tell us to be careful with the change. If we got back home with the wrong change, we'd have to go back to the store. We all actively participated in the everyday management of the household. We were aware of how much exactly was my father's salary, how much was the energy bill, and how much everything cost. In our house there wasn't money for luxuries like Nescau [the Brazilian variant of Nesquik]. But we had these African principles of collective collaboration. We had cousins who lived with us when their families went through difficulties. We ceded our beds for them and that's how things worked.

Concerning trauma, which is a specific concept in medicine, I think that we've been reconstructing ourselves since the fundamental event, which is slavery, and how it erased our humanity. It's as if, because of how we are mistreated, we are constantly re-experiencing the invasion and plunder of Africa. Our body is the territory. When someone says I can't be in the surgery room as a doctor in training, this person is saying I don't have the attributes of a recognizable human that allow me to be there. I'm not sure I can explain it well. To this day, there are spaces in which I'm not recognized as a medical doctor, even if I have my medical ID on me, or introduce myself as a medical doctor. That's because many people have never seen a doctor who looks like me. This estrangement started when I was in medical school where they'd never seen anyone like me, and it has followed me for more than twenty years. For me, this is the reenactment of that process of invasion and submission of the African territory which is today represented in my body.

In Rise Up or Die! we say that we experience a continuous sequela. From a process of violence that is enormous and multi-faceted, each sequela rebuilds itself. All our contemporary experiences are consequences of the slavery process. [We'll return to the concept of sequela in a later discussion.]

To conclude the earlier discussion on the health of the Black population, I think there was a debate in 2004, inside and outside the MNU, that focused on the effects of racism on people's health. Earlier, in 2001, a very important book by Fátima Oliveira, a Black doctor, was published, focusing on the health of the Black population.[36] In it, Oliveira analyzes eugenics and the first eugenics congress in Brazil in 1929. Oliveira points to the ways in which racial markers were related to processes of disease, but her insights are not taken up and elaborated upon. In 2004, I began having more access to such debates via the organizations I mentioned. From an institutional perspective, there was an ongoing national debate on neonatal triage, on sickle cell disease, and these were prominent in President Fernando Henrique Cardoso's federal administration, which made it a point to focus on the Black population. That's when I began to have a better conceptual sense of the pertinent questions.

I had lived it in my own skin: I began to understand why Black people had depression, suffered from alcoholism. Black people experience multiple forms of aggression from early on in their lives. For example, when someone called me a monkey, I'd get really sad. I'd go to a party where people would show me a bunch of bananas, and that would sadden me, but I had no understanding of what was going on. It would sadden me to hear other students tell me, "You won't be the Queen of Spring," and I'd get even more introspective. But I didn't recognize this as part of a broader constellation of suffering due to the mark of blackness. When I arrived in Bahia, I began participating in these discussions, and I got a better grasp of the underlying questions. In 2004, there were texts that discussed equity for the Black population, and in some of those there were linkages made between race, racism, well-being, and disease.

João: When you mention your family's concern in getting your mother out of the white family's house, it seems to me that you're addressing a fear of rape, which in turn suggests that sexual terror is a common experience for Black people.[37]

Andreia: I didn't want to talk about it directly, but yes. The driver who worked in the white family's house, an elder Black man who was very observant and dispensed advice, told my father that, as soon as possible, he should remove my mother from that house because the owner's sons were already observing my mother, who was very attractive. This was one of the most brutal situations, this vulnerability imposed by white men on Black women. I don't get too much into it to preserve my mother and my father's memory. But this was a recurring theme in our home where there were only Black women. We don't know exactly what happened, and if in fact my mother was subjected to anything—she has always been very quiet. Also, there had been in our family a history of sexual violence against one of my mother's older sisters. But I do agree that this is an important theme.

CHAPTER TWO
PHASES

In this chapter, Andreia and Hamilton summarize Rise Up's various phases during the last seventeen years, including moments of expansion and retraction.

THE CABULA MASSACRE: EVALUATING THE COLLECTIVE TRAJECTORY AND MOVING FORWARD

João: Can you please talk about the mobilization in the wake of the Cabula massacre? It seems like an important moment for Rise Up.

Hamilton: On February 6, 2015, the police killed twelve young people in the Cabula community. Providing support for the impacted families as best we could, we went through two weeks of indescribable hell. According to the press, the kids were killed while robbing a bank, but as soon as we arrived in the community, we realized the allegation made no sense because the bank was in the middle of their neighborhood. It never happens that people will rob a bank in their own community. The way the bodies were left, the marks on the ground—it all led us to believe the police had executed the young people.

The next day, we organized a protest march. Rede Globo national television, including a well-known reporter, Guilherme Belarmino, who to this day is our friend, accompanied us. Because he was with us, no one touched us. That day we were able to see the clothes the kids had worn, and the clothes of each one of them had bullet holes. We had to console the mothers, we had to recognize the bodies. There was a long legal process that we pushed forward and for which we had to gather the monetary and human resources.

The day after our march, we went to a meeting with the governor of the State of Bahia. It was a meeting to pacify Black people and to preemptively protect the governor. Andreia and I brought several Cabula neighborhood families whose members had been killed by the police, but the governor's staff only allowed Andreia and me to enter his cabinet. I objected and said they had to meet with the family members. That's when I noticed that inside the cabinet there were several Black people already, some of whom were activists celebrated in Brazil and the US, but who have never set foot in any of those neighborhoods. I know because I've been involved since the 1980s and I've never seen them in those areas. They circulate in universities, institutes, and foundations, but never in the streets. They had presents for the governor. "You're a bunch of scoundrels!" I told them. That was my internalized hatred coming out. Those so-called Black activists make it so that in Salvador you don't even need white people to do the dirty work. You don't even see the white people, their power is effective and invisible.

According to the investigation of the Public Prosecutor's Office, the Cabula massacre took place in the following manner. RONDESP military police officers went to the neighborhood to collect their bribe from drug traffickers.[1] For some reason, the dealers didn't want to pay the bribe and fired a shot, hitting one of the officers in the foot. In retaliation, they killed two youths, including Rodrigo, whose mother is a member of Rise Up or Die! Not satisfied, the officers went back into the community and rounded up and killed ten young people who were hanging out at a street corner, drinking and listening to music. They were seventeen- and eighteen-year-old kids. Twelve killed in total.

In our neighborhoods, when you see the RONDESP, you run. When I'm in the streets at night and I see them, I take off my shirt and I make a point of showing my hands are empty. When you permanently live with this kind of fear, that's how it works. Those kids ran when they saw the first group of police officers; they were ambushed by a second RONDESP group that shot them dead. To hide the bullet marks, the cops took off the kids' clothes and replaced them with army clothes. They also planted guns next to the kids to suggest they were about to rob a bank.

The only reason the Public Prosecutor's Office conducted an investigation was because Rise Up made a lot of noise. We brought the case to the Organization of American States (OAS).[2] At the OAS, they gave me twenty seconds to speak, but I ended up speaking for five minutes. When the OAS officials realized what I was denouncing something important, they let me talk, the red light didn't go off.

João: A decade after Rise Up or Die! is founded, what can you say about the mobilization you put together following the Cabula massacre? How does it demonstrate your accumulated organizing knowledge?

Hamilton: That was one of the toughest cases we faced, because of the sheer number of people killed on a single occasion. But it wasn't the worst in terms of terror. The worst was in Canabrava, in 2009, a small community on the outskirts of Salvador, where five people including three young brothers, aged twenty-two, twenty-three, and twenty-four, were executed by the police.[3] More than one hundred officers allegedly entered that community to avenge the death of one Civil Police officer, known as Ohara, who was notoriously corrupt.[4]

By the time the Cabula massacre took place, we were mature as an organization. We knew all the channels. We were articulated with many political allies, research institutions, media outlets, and legal forums at the local, state, national, and international levels. We had invented a way of doing Black politics that was based on our intentional miseducation. Back in the beginning, we were rough, we were purposefully loud and rude. Today, you know, I'm all polished, I'm cute even.

In the wake of the Cabula massacre, many people who had left Rise Up or Die! came back. The mothers of victims and residents of the affected community also joined us. In various Salvador areas, we created community nuclei of family and friends of victims of racist state violence and of incarcerated people.[5] It's important to note that we were able to do all of that despite inter-gang conflict. Every gang faction respected us. And we never had problems with intellectuals and academics. There are many former and current Rise Up members pursuing their masters and doctorates. The same is true of well-known Black artists who ask that their names not be revealed, but they consistently help with monetary contributions.

The Cabula massacre changed our perspective. Up to that point, we wanted to denounce and make visible the genocide of Black people in Brazil. We were successful, we made it visible worldwide. We articulated with organizations and peoples in several countries and continents, we organized marches in Salvador in which people from many parts of Brazil and from diverse nations took part. So we evaluated that Rise Up had fulfilled its mandate.

To discuss the next steps, in 2016 we put together a congress, the Encounter of Pan-Africanist Formation and Action (Encontro de Formação e Ação Pan-Africanista, EFOP). We had delegates from various states and main cities, including Rio de Janeiro and São Paulo. In it, we decided we couldn't be a campaign anymore, we had to be a political organization. We approved our bylaws. Instead of making demands to the state and society, we were going to focus on concrete action: the construction of spaces of resistance, solidarity, and happiness. Those spaces would be cultural centers, schools, community gardens, banks, communitarian restaurants for unhoused people—all of which we accomplished. In 2016, we built the Winnie Mandela school; we had the "factory of dreams," which was an initiative with formerly incarcerated people who sold candy (*sonho,* the candy, literally means "dream") and other snacks on the streets; they were able to pay their rent doing that. We had a community garden. We had land; and now we're trying to get that started again.

Importantly, our political organization was going to be horizontal and its ultimate coordination done by the women-only Comando Vital. We know that women are the ones who make everything happen. Many of our brothers, as advanced as they are, did not accept the women's leadership. There was a lot of tension around that.

João: Regarding that transition from campaign (2005–2014) to political organization (2015 to the present), can you please talk about who were the people present in each phase?

Hamilton: In 2005, when we constituted ourselves as a campaign, we had eighteen organizations under the Rise Up or Die! umbrella. There were groups of high school and college students, dissident Black movement members, and people from various favelas and communities. The leadership was basically Andreia,

Marcos Alessandro, who's a history professor, Leone Zumbi, a Black youth who had contacts with radical organizers in Spain, and me. At thirty-four, I was the oldest of the group. We already felt isolated vis-a-vis the Black movement, but we engaged in many solidarity activities. We denounced several acts of police brutality and killings. Back then our prison activities were already strong—we were well known throughout the entire state penitentiary system. We were well known inside the prisons and in the streets.

In 2012, feeling that we needed to develop our own concept of safety, we organized the Encontro Nacional por um Outro Modelo de Segurança Pública (National Encounter for Another Model of Public Security, ENPOSP). This conference was in opposition to the first state-sponsored Conferência Nacional de Segurança Pública (National Conference on Public Security, CONSEG).

In that same year, we participated in an event at the University of São Paulo Law School called "Tribunal Popular: O Estado Brasileiro no Banco dos Réus" (Popular Tribunal: The Brazilian State as Defendant).[6] To prepare for it, we gathered family members of victims of state violence and several nongovernmental organizations. When this debate first started, it was dominated by white people and human rights NGOs. We changed that and said, "No whites are going to speak about and for us and our suffering." We demanded that the mothers of victims speak. Soon thereafter we were called racists.

At the Popular Tribunal we presented the Salvador cases of Kleber Álvaro, who was shot several times and became paraplegic, and that of Negro Blul, who was killed—both victims of the state military police. We put the cases on trial, with me as the judge. I argued that, if it was a popular tribunal, then I could be the judge. There were actual judges in the event, including one that is close to Rise Up, Maurício Brasil. It was for that event that a famous musician, Carlinhos Brown, paid the airfare for some of the mothers of those killed by the police.

Following that event, we articulated with Global Justice, Mães de Maio (Mothers of May), MNU, and several other organizations, to have the ENPOSP in Salvador. Rise Up or Die! would host it. At the time we had a great relationship with the Public Prosecutor's Office, whose chief prosecutor accepted our ways of doing politics and she understood well the white liberal women of the human rights NGOs. We asked for her office's support and she agreed. We didn't want any money, just help with accommodations for the victims' mothers—we wanted them to stay in decent hotels. The Public Prosecutor's Office funded the accommodations for the mothers. We told the white people that we could only offer them to stay in hostels, and if they preferred they could pay their own stay. It all worked out very well, it was well attended. We did it in the School of Architecture at the University of Bahia. Angela Davis and Pataxó Indians gave keynotes.

In retrospect, I think it was an error to include other organizations and white people. I've never said it like this. There was a white psychologist from São Paulo who wanted to speak. We didn't allow her to speak and we said, "You already said enough about us, you wrote several books, why don't you let other people talk, people who actually went through the violence and brutality we're talking about?"

Predictably, there were all kinds of accusations against us—that we're uncouth, sexist (because we silenced the white woman), rude. Several Black people rushed to console the white person. They accused us of purposefully creating discomfort regarding the accommodations. But for us, it was all about prioritizing decent accommodations for the mothers who had lost their children, to treat them with dignity, like full human beings, and actually treat them well for a change. So it was a mistake to invite white people; it was a mistake also to share our deepest emotions, pains, and fears with them. I think it's fine for white people to be allies, for them to collaborate with us on specific programs, and they can even be in attendance of certain events. But please, they can't tell us how and why we feel.

João: What do you think were the positive outcomes of the ENPOSP?

Hamilton: It helped us strengthen our networks with other Black collectives. It allowed us to discuss genocide beyond Salvador. We added to the discussion the entire Northeast region of Brazil, which is often neglected because it is assumed that all that matters happens only in Rio de Janeiro and São Paulo. Unfortunately this wrong assumption is still prevalent. We heard a variety of analyses and narratives, which helped us further elaborate our agenda, and that led to us becoming more solidly international. The encounter's proposals—there were so many that we'd need several book volumes to cover them—were very generative in terms of how they were practical and implementable. It created a network of protection that went beyond the organizations since many state authorities participated.

João: Can you talk about Rise Up's initial expansion in Salvador and beyond?

Hamilton: The first expansion process was in Salvador, we went inside the communities. The traditional Black movement only operated in downtown. We made it a point to go to the most distant communities, the most violent and impoverished areas. At that point we also had a discussion about masculinities, which was a way to talk with the men. We cooked with them, and then we talked. We had cinema shows, we had spoken word groups. I remember going to a distant neighborhood, Alto do Coqueirinho. We had to go through a narrow bridge over a creek, and our activity was in a pool shack. Later we expanded to the interior of the state, we hooked up with Fred Aganju's group made up of students of the Federal University of the Recôncavo da Bahia in the city of Cachoeira. We collaborated with that group and Fred joined Rise Up or Die! After that we went to another city in the southern part of the Bahia state, Ilhéus, and we had a debate about land: we discussed taking over land, agricultural techniques, and we decided to plant cacao and export it to the US. We weren't able to secure containers for international sales, but we sold it to other places in Brazil.

We had our first march against the genocide of Black people in 2006, and the subsequent marches were always well attended. We stopped traffic and took over the downtown area. We had yearly marches between 2006 and 2015, uninterrupted. Initially they were marches titled Against the Genocide of Black people.

In 2013, we decided to make the march an international protest against the genocide of Black people. We called it the International March Against the Genocide of Black People. We did the international march for three years.

We traveled the country to articulate with different groups and organizations, some of which had marches in cities like Belo Horizonte, Rio de Janeiro, São Paulo, Recife, and Porto Alegre. In 2013, the left thought we wanted to march against the president of the Workers' Party at the time, Dilma Rousseff, who was under a lot of pressure due to protests against her all over the country. We also traveled internationally, to Spain, Germany, Switzerland, England, Guatemala, and Colombia. We insisted that our march was independent and was to protest the genocide of Black people. People from several countries either participated directly, organized their own local protests, or sent their support. It was a very powerful moment. We had over sixty thousand people in the streets in total—imagine doing that without any kind of financial resources. One of the consequences of that march was the creation of Rise Up or Die! nuclei throughout the country.

Between 2013–2015, we traveled internationally to articulate with groups in Europe and the Americas. We wanted to denounce genocide, which was a concept not often used to refer to Black people's suffering. We adapted the concept from the Brazilian penal code. But for us it was never about making a name for ourselves, getting prizes and recognition.

In 2014, we started doing the annual marches against the genocide of Black people only in the communities; we don't go to downtown anymore. We think it no longer makes sense to say we're needlessly dying. It should be known by now. We want to explore other methods, other approaches. We want to destroy things. There's no way to reform the social structures that kill us. Some people come to Rise Up wanting to change us, wanting to make us more polished and recognizable, but that never works and we tell them to leave.

By then, in Brazil the discussion of genocide was widespread, there were studies about it, and legislative forums at every level were debating the theme. We had a face-to-face meeting with Joaquim Barbosa, the first Black president of the Supreme Federal Court, who opposed our perspective. He said, "It's bad to call yourselves Rise Up [Reaja] because it's like you want people to kill each other." I said, "No, it's similar to what happened to you here in the Supreme Court when a colleague of yours, Gilmar Mendes, offended you, and you reacted as if to say you didn't fear him. This is what we mean; it doesn't mean we go out and start killing people." At that point we used to say, "Don't beat them up, just rise up!" [não precisa bater, reaja!].

For that, and of course many other frictions, people created a dislike of us, even indignation. They cut relations with us and isolated us. It was heavy. Rise Up imploded shortly thereafter, hundreds of militants left. Some of those who left said, "I need to live my life; I need to pay my rent." Following the Cabula massacre, others left for the government, and they created an organization that also wore black shirts and promised to distribute basic needs kits widely in the community. We had no way of competing with those folks who had access to state, foundations, and private resources, who flew up and down the country.

There's always tension in Rise Up or Die! We routinely deal with people who just left prison; women who work and take care of several children, who are often left alone at home. We have people who steal, who sell and use drugs. We deal with young people who have unprotected sex. So it's a lot of problems, a lot of terror, and not much of a financial structure. That's our reality. Life in our organization is difficult. We're not in an office, we're not in the university. We see our people getting arrested, we see houses being swept by the rains, and we really can't deal with all of that.

We were unable to attend to our own activists' needs, and most people left. That's what I mean when I say we retreated—we were just unable to carry on.

When we retreated, the deaths continued. The state government created PATAMO (Patrulhamento Tático-Móvel, a subunit of the Shock Police Battalion). We have to ask ourselves, and we have to ask those who are in the Workers' Party: did Bolsonaro really start this disgrace against Black people, or does it precede Bolsonaro? We're not saying Bolsonaro is a saint—he's awful, as is his government. But it wasn't his government that started the widespread killing of our people. We have to ask the people who are in the Workers' Party administration, who travel the world talking about all the good they've done, what community are they a part of? Where were they when the youths in Cabula were assassinated? What about when the thousands of others were routinely killed, where were they? When we were threatened, where were they? Instead of pressuring the government, they just told us to vote for their candidates. They keep telling us that we don't know how to do politics—and that's true, we really don't. We know how to survive in a gigantic prison that is Brazil.

During the COVID-19 pandemic, we denounced the deaths of several youths: ten-year-old Joel, then Micael, then Ryan; we were able to pressure the Bahia government to implement a policy allowing women who were pregnant or had children aged twelve or younger to serve their sentences at home; the same for people who had previous life-threatening conditions and older people. We also pressured so that incarcerated people could vote. We were able to maintain our headquarters, our school. We're planning ahead; we have projects that provide health care access, education opportunities, and we have a food program. So we're preparing a leap. Our retreat was for us to prepare.

João: Can you talk about these different phases of expansion and retreat?

Hamilton: We had several moments of expansion and retraction. When we first emerged in 2005, we had more than three hundred people in our events; then, in 2006, we had thirteen people. After that, we intensified our work in prisons and in communities; we traveled; we wrote analysis papers; and we grew again, which culminated in 2008 when we had a Popular Encounter for Another Model of Public Safety.

Then, in 2014, we came to the understanding that the way we did our denouncing wasn't working anymore; that's when the deaths of the youths at Cabula took place. We organized a great march, but the internal contradictions were evident. There were lots of divisions among the Bahia folks, and the same was true with members in other states. There were competing factions that wanted to take over Rise Up. There were Pan-Africanists— we called them seated Africans because they were mostly scholars who had positions in the government and/or in the university— who were out of touch with reality. There were anarchists, who've always supported us; younger Pan-Africanists who until recently were Christian evangelicals and all of a sudden wanted to change the world ignoring everything that happened before them.

There were many people who arrived in Rise Up who had serious issues to contend with: the person who was incarcerated while attempting to rob a car; the one who hated someone else; the one who was depressed; the one who did drugs excessively. We had to administer all of that. That's when we established the Comando Vital, and we established rules and criteria, which antagonized many people who subsequently left. After a while, other people came in and people are still coming back. We had to take several steps back. But we remember the words of an incarcerated South African activist: when a goat retreats, it does so to prepare an attack. We did the same: we retreated to prepare for an attack.

João: Can you please talk about wanting to destroy things—destroy what exactly, and for what?

Hamilton: For us, the Brazilian state cannot be reformed. The dominant intelligentsia says there's structural racism. So if that's the case, how are you going to reform it? How can you adapt to racism, how can you live in that kind of structure? We need to destroy this Brazilian society and create alternatives of power. How do you do it? We're going to create our own state—at first within the existing state. We're going to retake the land and create free communities. We're going to create schools, our own banks. That's what I mean by destroying the Brazilian society. But this also involves destroying current understandings of human relations, sexuality, family, and even militancy. Our job is to destroy all these Western notions.

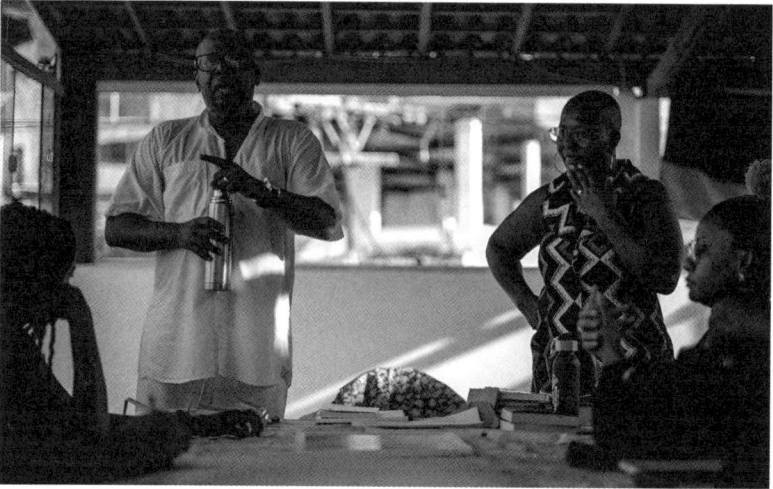

CHAPTER THREE

FUNDAMENTALS

In this chapter, Andreia and Hamilton focus on additional concepts that are fundamental to the practice of Rise Up or Die!

Hamilton: When Rise Up first started, we read a book by Cornell West, *Race Matters*, that had a chapter on Black rage. We identified with it. The majority of Black people have rage. Rage and hatred are related. I have a friend who was born and raised in Curuzu, he never left. He had a hatred of white people, which is common in that area. The white people's city has always been the rich neighborhoods with the nice beaches; they have swimming pools, they have all the best things. We'd go there in a clandestine way, we jumped over walls to go to those beaches. And we stole. We wanted to upset them. We knew we weren't equal to them, that's where the hatred came from. All of my family had that hatred—they told us (the younger ones) to be careful with white people. I have written about this hatred. One of my reflections says something like, "Everything in São Paulo is new, everything in São Paulo is modern. The president's suit is how Black people are killed." My hatred is ancient.

CREATIVE HATRED

João: Could you say more about this hatred? It's a sentiment that's not often discussed in Black political formations.

Hamilton: Anger is a common experience—it is frequent for me. When you talk about anger, and when you talk with anger, you are left out of spaces of debate, you get shunned. Even the people who like and support me, they say things like, "Hamilton would be ideal to invite to talk about this topic, but he's too angry." To be angry is on par with our skin color. The blacker one is, the angrier one is. Black women are angry. I studied anger; I read Audre Lorde. When the Zapatistas came to Brazil, they stressed dignified anger—they, too, were inspired by Lorde, who tried to explain her own anger as opposed to hatred and white women's guilt.

We needed a concept different from anger. I developed my own concept of creative hatred. Most of what Rise Up accomplished is related to the hatred we have of being in this city. There's a lot of talk about love, lots of events and texts on it. Recently, an online live event focused on love, and everyone was hugging everyone else. They had African clothes made in China, sold in Brazil. Then there's a related concept of self-care, which empties the collective and puts all the responsibility on the individual. If you're not well, it's because you don't know how to take care of yourself.

We fed from the hatred we felt each time someone was abused, each time someone was brutalized, each time we buried someone. In our study groups and in our extensive networks, which includes the anarchists—who have great respect for us—and the Zapatistas, we developed a shared concept of anger, drawing from Audre Lorde's reflections.[1] But the main sentiment we had wasn't anger, it was far more radical and outrageous. We felt hatred. We didn't want our hatred to be inside of us, bottled up, used against us. We needed to put it out, white people needed to feel our hatred.

Our pedagogy of hatred returns the hatred to those who direct it to us; we return it via actions that strengthen us. Which part of the Black movement in Salvador has a copy machine that's used to copy the books college students have to read and can't afford to buy? No one but us. We have a school! Many of the Black organizations ask the government for space, for resources, for recognition—they're always asking for this and that. We just take over what is ours, we just do what is needed, we don't ask. That's creative hatred. That's a form of love. We love ourselves and one another.

In Rise Up or Die! we say that we must have love among ourselves. Toward our enemy, we need to employ hatred because it's impossible to experience slavery as we still do and not be marked by hatred in our body. In therapy—and it took me a long time to accept that I needed it—frequently I talked about rejection, about not being able to recognize myself, accept myself, all of which was related to not feeling like I was human enough. I ask myself, how did we manage to survive for so long? Throughout my life, I've had so much hatred directed at me, it has everything to do with my racial experience—how white people hate me, how I deal with white people, and how I deal with Black people who love white people more than they love their own people.

Our approach in Rise Up created different possibilities. People in prisons, in communities—and here I mean communities that are armed, where young kids who are part of the drug economy carry assault rifles: we tell them that we can channel our internalized hatred in a different way, we can be creative. If you're pointing all those weapons to your own community, then they're useless.

For me, Salvador is the largest laboratory of Black destruction. You look at São Paulo, there's hatred there, it's palpable everywhere, everyone's on edge; there and in Rio, the youth is armed, they train their weapons not only at other Black people, but also at the state, regardless if it's a good or bad tactic, or if the final objective is good or bad. But here in Salvador there's this sense of happiness, of racial harmony fulfilled. You go to Pelourinho, downtown, and you see white people being treated well, and Black boys, Black girls, they want to interact with European people because it's a great way to solve their family's economic struggles. I know several young people who marry white Europeans who don't have good jobs in Europe, who never went to college. They leave their Black partners who work, who study, whose house is well organized and clean, who bought the TV, the couch—and they swap them for the white European. When they arrive in Europe, after a month or so, they feel the hatred the European has for them, the hatred their family has for them. They separate and, out of pride, stay there, constantly struggling financially and emotionally.

Black people have historically developed two personas. We have one for whites: in front of them, we show our teeth, we say "sir," we hug, we laugh. But when we're out of their sight, we hate them, we call them names. From early on, we developed hatred towards whites because we knew they took everything from us. The community knows the police serve whites. Black people know that, if you're with whites, the chance of being stopped by the police is much lower. Here in my neighborhood, which is overwhelmingly Black, there are a couple of bars owned by whites. The police don't even bother going there; they go straight to the Black-owned bars.

Even if your grasp of racial dynamics is minimal, it's impossible to miss the widespread, multifaceted and quotidian hatred against Black people, and it's impossible not to internally develop hatred against this situation. So what did Rise Up do? We appropriated this hatred and transformed it into a tool. We had to use the hatred to denounce the systematic killing of Black people; we hoped it resonated with supporters to join us.

In the beginning of Rise Up or Die! I remember a group of us reading the newspaper, and we commented on seven deaths of Black people here, ten deaths there. We asked ourselves, why was there no indignation about the deaths of Black people? Why don't we get upset? That's when we decided to begin a project of analytical introspection and to confront fear. The perspective of hatred helps us confront fear. Fear is a structure that is placed inside of us, and it makes us backtrack, cede ground. When we started to do our "political performances" in spaces that were dominated by whites who talked about our collective disgrace, there was no one talking about public security from the perspective of the ghetto. The whites who spoke for us had the perspective of the panopticon, they were looking from above, they were not in our neighborhoods, in the street corners, they were not in the Coroner's Office to identify the dead bodies, they were not in the hospitals, they were not protesting in front of the police; they were reading books, journals.

We had a different approach. Luiza Bairros perhaps put it best when she said we invented bad manners in politics. We crashed into meetings, we didn't ask if we could participate. Bairros said it not as a critique, but as in, "It was about time!"

Hatred is a tool because it confronts fear, and it confronts oblivion. On the first anniversary of the mass killing of Black youth in Cabula, we reiterated the need for embracing creative hatred, which is different from the Zapatista's creative anger. We're talking about something else, we're saying we're in an open air prison, like the Angola prison in the US. There may not be obvious fences, but we're being surveilled all the time. When I go out, I don't know when a cop will put a gun to my face, like it happened several times. This great prison is forgotten by the meek people who engage in the race relation debates. They forgot the weight of the lash, of slavery, they forgot how slavery impacted our own constitution—we can't escape it, there's no therapy that soothes the pain.

Creative hatred is not the hatred of a Black person pointing the gun to another Black person; it is not the hatred against Black women that manifests when we say, "They're so full of anger," "They're so demanding." Creative hatred is what makes you build new things, as we've done in the last seventeen years. We've been confrontational, and we don't respect institutions. We call out white people's hatred towards us, we externalize the hatred that we've been subjected to. Someone may be the best white person in the world, but they will inevitably manifest hatred against us, unconsciously at least. So what do we do? Do we oppose hatred with kisses, with hugs? We decided to embrace hatred and confrontation.

Instead of self-destructing, instead of destroying our community, instead of smashing public phones, instead of damaging bus stops, creative hatred moves us to strengthen our collectives. There are countless events on love, self-care—for us that doesn't work because what's needed is respect for our community, our people. We are not able to love everyone if we're not even able to love ourselves. We will learn how to love ourselves.

We express love in many ways. For example, we have a project called Theory About Us. Every month, we call the community to reflect on ourselves via literature, poetry, cooking, capoeira. This weekend we'll have rap music and spoken word. We'll have conversations on masculinity—we don't even know if that's how we're going to call it. We'll have Black men discussing masculinity, sexuality, violence, and hatred. This is profound love.

Nobody likes us; we're the most disdained people on earth. People think we're violent, that we don't respect women. In Rise Up, we're constantly addressing our emotions; we're addressing our community, what we're eating; we're addressing our health. We're already doing much of that, and we're going to do more, we're going to expand our activities. We'll begin with fifty people; maybe only twenty will stay for the entire duration, maybe only five. But we don't give up. This is how we express our hatred against racism.

People who see differently than us, they seek to appropriate power in governance at the local, state, and national levels. They don't understand that communitarian action creates autonomous governance in our own territory. Meanwhile, Black people are trying to get into the official government structure. Instead, they could be helping build Black autonomous communities. Of course we could not accomplish all of this in seventeen years. But we're not giving up.

João: Andreia, can you tell us how hatred became central in Rise Up's program and its public presentation? Where does it come from?

Andreia: Our feet have been in the mud—we've been active where life happens, where Black people live and die. This is critical and informs the decisions we've made over the years. As a collective, we recognize we're permanently experiencing violence and brutality. There's no negotiating, and there's no way to bring some relief if not through confrontation. Death is constantly around us: violent death, premature death, physical death, emotional death, structural death. Also the death of belonging. Constantly faced with death and with our demise as a people, we understand that radicality in our actions is absolutely necessary: radicality in the construction of our autonomy and of a power system in which we are central and we determine our next steps.

Radicality in our existence means that we won't flinch, we won't give ground to or negotiate with the enemy because we are part of a multitude who shares an experience.

Because he's an activist with a long trajectory, Hamilton is more visible, but Rise Up's radicality defines our children as well as all those who have been with us for longer. For us, faced with routine brutal state assassinations, like those of the twelve youths in Cabula, with frequent police kidnappings and disappearances of Black people, it's impossible to stay passive. We seek a radical stance vis-a-vis a system that criminalizes us, stops and arrests us for no reason, that doesn't provide minimum conditions for our existence. Our radicality stems from recognizing we have no guarantees of basic human dignity.

We are inspired by Winnie Mandela, for me one of our greatest references, a Black woman who chose a radical response while experiencing similar dire circumstances. There's no negotiation, there's nothing to offer except the hatred of which we are the object. What can you offer when you learn that a Black person had their head cut off by a police officer while alive? In this context, there's no scenario in which I can imagine having a decent life—direct and indirect brutality put us in a situation in which a radical response, which is to search the deep roots of current events, is the necessary mode by which we organize ourselves.

There's the danger of illusion: because you may have a good pair of shoes, because you may have food or nice clothes, you might think that this overwhelming violence is not going to find you. But it will find you, and we have countless examples of how it happens. We constantly relive the brutality of slavery, in myriad ways. We're followed when we go to the store, we're constantly at risk of being stopped and brutalized by the police; our presence in spaces of relative privilege is always questioned. Our radicality stems from the constant negation of our humanity.

João: Why do you think the emphasis on hatred is not taken up by other Black organizations? Based on what you said, it seems that the avoidance of hatred is related to a perspective that avoids considering as enemies the Brazilian state and society. It seems to me that for other Black organizations, and for most of the white left, the state is an adversary, not an enemy. For them, the state is considered a bureaucratic apparatus and social networks that you can find your way into, you can adjust, you can domesticate for your own needs. What I hear in Rise Up or Die! is that the state is the enemy, we don't negotiate with it, we oppose and confront it. Why do you think this bothers other organizations so much?

Andreia: This is interesting, and directs us toward the government's agenda for Black people, especially the popular democratic agenda of the Workers' Party (PT). This agenda was a response to the high numbers of premature death of Black youth. PT understood that it was a process of extermination of Black youth. In 2012, to address the disproportionate early death of Black youth, the federal government started a program called Juventude Viva (Youth Alive).[2] The resources were limited, and focused on seminars in air conditioned rooms, things like that.

From the very beginning, Rise Up or Die! termed the phenomenon a genocide of Black people. This made people uncomfortable. If we say there's a genocide in course, then we are also saying that as Black people we don't belong, we're not considered Brazilian citizens.

The debate on racial hatred dislocates the white power structure built on the myth of racial democracy that promotes a type of integration to which we Black people have to submit, as do Indigenous peoples. When we articulate antiblack hatred, when we say genocide of Black people, we're dislocating this entire power structure—which, by the way, also suggests that anyone can occupy any position in society. It's unsurprising that when we focus on antiblack hatred, we are blamed for inciting the hatred, that we are separatists, that we don't want to build with other people. We're told that, to focus on hatred makes it impossible for society to reach equality, to which we say we don't seek equality because in this country equality means equality for white people who want to continue enjoying their privileges while maintaining our oppression. To speak of antiblack hatred is to speak of our presence, which is really an absence, and ultimately it is about challenging white privilege.

João: If Black people don't belong, if antiblack hatred is prevalent, and the state is the enemy, what is Rise Up proposing?

Andreia: In 2016, we had a campaign, "Don't Vote, Rise Up!," which called for a boycott of the elections. It came from our understanding that our participation in electoral campaigns and elections ended up benefiting the same groups.[3] If we look at all the political parties, there's no specific proposal in which we Black people and our principles are guiding the debate. Historically, political parties have had Black nuclei, Black working groups, things like that. But what we propose is different. We want to build political proposals with the recognition of our place in the world and with our own concepts. We maintain that, as it stands, the electoral system is not able to respond to our demands.

We can't be treated as a subgroup because we're the majority of the population; we've had fundamental contributions to the existence and richness of this country. We don't want just a share; we want to autonomously redirect our collective trajectory: this is where we came from, this is where we are at, and this is where we want to go. The current political system is not able to do that: it cannot respond to our demands and it cannot incorporate our projects of society. Therefore, we understand that we need to continue building our projects in community, our struggle is a communitarian one. As Winnie Mandela said, communitarian organization is not enough; we need communitarian struggle. We have to articulate all that we've created over the years. In order to build what is possible, we start with our own institutions, like the Winnie Mandela school. That's why it's so important to discuss communitarian care practices, communitarian safety practices—how do we protect our communities when faced with a public security system that only sees us as the enemy.

Our practice of construction seeks to guarantee a communitarian process. To advance, we need a base, we need land—which we have—and we need to have institutions built according to our own perspective. Now we can discuss what else we want to build: how do we confront our enemy, what strategies do we use, what technologies do we employ? The struggle is immense, and it is demeaning. Often, the state reduces important Black activists to nothing. How can we continue to believe in a system that doesn't recognize our capacity to build, our potential? For us, it's impossible to believe that the enemy can generate any kind of substantial recognition of our humanity. It can be deflating to reach this conclusion, but we continue to seek communitarian construction. It's not easy. There are many technologies of seduction. One of them is the narrative that we can be anything we want, and we can occupy any space. Real life shows us that is just not possible.

A DEEP BLACK SADNESS

João: In previous conversations, you mentioned the centrality of a deep sadness in the collective experience of Black people. Can you please elaborate?

Hamilton: I joined the Black movement more than thirty years ago. Our trajectory in this country is soaked in sadness. The word sadness doesn't quite capture it. I don't know what other word to use. Back then, the Black movement called it *banzo*—after a carnival bloc that was called "Melô do Banzo." It's more like melancholia that started in the Middle Passage. It's something heavy. I hear it in Black carnival songs, which are often sad. There's a composer in Salvador named Suka, he has a song that says, "I came from Africa, and I brought music," and it's sang with sadness. Mano Brown, another composer I admire, has a poem that defines banzo: "Dead leaf in the wind, I'm useless. Dying slowly, that's how I feel." And then he says, "I see Black people in all corners of this big world, all of them sad."[4] Mano Brown is about my age, and I think we see Black people similarly.

With relation to the carnival blocs, imagine you're fifteen, sixteen years old, and you want to have fun. But then you hear this: "To salute my sentiments, mother, only love can help us against all the meanness of the human race . . . Go Ilê Ayiê, fight for freedom and with your truth kill hypocrisy." You hear the sadness. It's as if all our expressions tell us there's a pain that's tearing from inside your chest. We live a profound sadness, that's what I think banzo is.

It's very difficult to shake off this deep sadness. I wonder if this sadness is a result of the historical and political process in which we're immersed. We're in a strange land, we're constantly told we don't belong, regardless of who we are or the social status we have. I ask myself if this sadness is actually depression. You may be in the middle of drumming, but you'll hear melancholy. Similar to the blues in the US, both in instrumental music and vocals. I'm trying to find this sentiment in the arts and in culture, but it's difficult to name this deep sorrow.

I think it has to do with how our humanity was destroyed, and then how we found ourselves trying to get it back. But often this attempt at reclaiming humanity comes together with trying to be as close to whiteness as possible. It's a permanent contradiction because when you're amongst whites, you immediately know you don't belong. Somehow they will tell you their spaces are not for you and that they don't want you.

For us, the best space to be is with other Black people. By choice, we live in the Engenho Velho de Brotas neighborhood, which is majority Black. If we lived in Pituba, which is majority white, I think we'd feel sad all the time.

All of this defines our activism in Rise Up or Die! This deep sadness is quite present. For example, when we started to see the dead as subjects, beyond the numbers, it became more concrete. To be sure, there had been previous awareness and analyses of violent deaths of Black people. But it's different when you actually go where the deaths took place, when you go to the Coroner's Office, when you attend the funerals, when you talk to the victims' mothers, their siblings. It's even worse when you go to funerals in the poorest cemeteries in Salvador, which are a multitude of vertical drawers. It's usually a lone mother crying and evangelical people consoling.

The sadness in the cemetery scenes is also profound because, by contrast, here in Bahia death is part of an African ritual; death is usually a festive celebration. My father's death was a celebration: there was samba, jokes, singing, card games. In Candomblé, death is a celebration ritual in which we talk with the deceased, we tell stories, we laugh, and we cry only when we leave the cemetery. However, the experience of state violence and terrorism changed this festive approach to death. When you kill a child or an adolescent in their most exuberant phase, you take away the mother's will to live. How many times have we met mothers with empty gazes? This sadness has no cure, and it's one that is widespread in our communities.

I observe the men—in a few days we'll be having another seminar with Black men, as we've been doing all along. I notice our behavior in bars, in soccer stadiums, and it's a lot of sadness. That's why they drink so much, they need to anesthetize themselves. They can't bear to live in this reality, which is too heavy. Some people will point out that white men also drink. But white men are already realized ontologically in their subjectivity; they're born that way. They're born as people who can succeed, who will not be randomly approached by the police, who are not a priori considered angry and uncouth, who are not seen as walking phalluses. I walk a lot around my own neighborhood and others like it. I observe what happens in prisons. I see this deep sadness everywhere, which I also feel. But I'd rather face this reality sober than anesthetized.

Sobriety has its downsides, though. You realize that you can't move in the city freely, you can't go into a restaurant without everyone looking at you, you can't get into a class in college without being invisible. I remember many moments of profound sadness—for example, when I lost my job in Minas Gerais, and I had to send my sons to Salvador. I found myself alone during Christmas, I was depressed, in bed. Was that only about my personal experience or was it related to centuries of stigmatization? I'm at a loss, I don't think I can even speak anymore.

João: Thank you. How were you able to channel, or transform, this deep sadness into a political program? For a lot of people, this sadness is paralyzing, it can become clinical depression, and the person is not able to get up, as you described. How did it become a spring for collective action that doesn't accept the imposed conditions on Black people?

Hamilton: Participating in a political organization allowed me to have an alternative perspective. The experience of deep sadness is motivation for me to continue engaging in collective projects that seek change. And again, women were fundamental because they articulated a critique of men's behaviors. Some of us men heard it, and it became an internal call against inertia and ignorance. There's nothing special about what we do. And unfortunately there's still a lot of men's violence against women, gays, and trans people, both in the Black movement and in Rise Up. Some of this is people being depressed, which is widespread. We keep trying to reach those men, to talk with them, and link them to psychological services. At the Bahia Federal University, for example, there's a psychologist who conducts group sessions and focuses specifically on the issues I mentioned. We strive to capacitate activists who are prepared to at least deal internally with the deep sadness and pain.

João: It sounds like this deep sadness has a side to it that's creative and productive—it's not only paralysis, but it's also movement. It's as if this deep sadness requires a personal and collective reaction, otherwise the depression is individualized and the person is rendered useless, and can even commit suicide.

Hamilton: Exactly. It paralyzes, but you can take the first step towards building with your community. We're going through a tough time right now. I was planning a festival here in the neighborhood, which is where there's the greatest concentration of traditional Candomblé houses—*terreiros*—and it's also where Mestre Bimba created the regional capoeira.[5] Right across the street there's the Castro Alves performance/theater house, totally abandoned. We announced the festival using the word "Black" in the publicity as often as we could. People resisted it and attendance was poor.

It's frustrating. This area is a food desert, yet there are giant supermarkets white people own. We could be planting our own food, we could be implementing a series of improvements in our community. But people don't care. Also, activism has become a business. Well-known Black activists are now on TV. They invent terms that are hollow. They do ads for the alcohol industry. The activism that I learned was all about community services, like the Black Panthers did, like Steve Biko did. I'm not saying you shouldn't have a business, that you shouldn't make money. I'm saying you could dedicate one or two hours of your life to collective actions because when you do so, the community improves and so do the lives of those who are there. Today, the majority of the activists concentrates on the electoral process, which is about getting votes. There's no political formation that allows for a gaze that focuses on what's around us.

In Rise Up, we have our biweekly seminars, sometimes monthly, and with a lot of difficulty we try to provide a space for that kind of political formation in which we invite scholars who focus on relevant authors and concepts. It's been challenging, but we won't give up. We've been successful before, we created powerful institutions like Candomblé, quilombos, and now it's our turn and we're here. We're here.

João: Do you see a connection between Black love and this deep sadness?

Hamilton: Black love goes beyond the contemporary struggle. I was raised in a rural community, even though it was in Salvador: there was no asphalt, it was mostly mud houses, cows and horses around, and no one went hungry. There was a barter system. The community members took care of each other. If there was a child far away from their home, it was understood that a neighbor or anyone in the community was authorized to bring the child back to their house. So it's not about bourgeois love, but it was a deep care for one another. I lived in that environment. We were all alike physically; we were more or less in the same economic situation, some poorer, some richer, but there was a sharing of resources.

Black love is part of our DNA, and it often shows as a sadness. We're forced to live close to one another. In Curuzu, we had the consistent experience of loving Black people, who for us were never ugly, were never outside of the norm. My first girlfriend was dark as the night. Our love for one another has always been there. These days there's an attempt to reaffirm Black beauty, but the damage has been done. When we left our community of Curuzu, and we saw white people at the beach, we thought they had super powers. We saw them as our enemies. If you touched a white person, you could be arrested. I was watching a documentary on a famous Black singer of the 1950s, and when she dips her feet in a hotel's swimming pool, they empty the pool. It was no different for us. I remember jumping over the wall of private clubs, and we'd get in the pool. Everyone knew we didn't belong. There was a lot of anger and hatred towards us when we did that, and they'd beat us and they'd lock us up. Imagine how those things affect your mind. How am I going to have any kind of harmonious relationship with a white person? I have many white collaborators, white friends, but I know my limits with them. Also, there are the light-skinned people who decided to be Black. That's the same kind of people who came for me at the swimming pool, beat me up, tortured me. Even the Salvador mayor is now self-declared Black. I see many light-skinned people who discovered racism in college. But I look at their social media and everyone around them is white. They can't deal with us because we're Black, we're loud, we're rude, we like to party. We intrude in other people's lives, like when there's a woman passing by and she's not holding the child's hand, we say "Miss, hold on to the children." That's common everywhere there's Black people, it's a civilization trait.

When the antiracism debate arrived, apparently everyone became antiracist, and now they want to teach us what racism and its effects are. There's people now talking about whiteness. We've been talking about it for years. There's a local militant, Landê, who insists that, in debates, white people need to state how they feel being white, they need to tell us how they feel in a country where a Black person will be destroyed in order to protect a white person. We don't need to hear about racism from white people. But now whiteness has become a source of income inside universities, and white people have become specialists. And they think their whiteness qualifies them to talk with us about racism. The other day there was someone on social media saying that Black people need to struggle more.

I observe the men in my family, where, over many generations and as a result of our religion, there has been considerable feminine power. I worship the great mothers. Yet I saw my father languish: he was a great artist. He was known as Antônio do

Banjo, he played the guitar and many other instruments. I witnessed him disappear from of our lives, like so many other men. This is also part of the profound sadness.

A COLLECTIVE ARMOR

Andreia: I must say that this conversation is impacting me deeply. [Andreia means the recording sessions as a whole.]

João: Can you say why?

Andreia: Because I had to revisit all the hatred that I experienced, that I always felt directed at me, but for which I didn't have a name and couldn't quite locate. I knew it had to do with my physical appearance. It was very brutal to relive all of that. This concept, that, in order to survive, we need to keep reinventing ourselves and wear an armor so that we can go through all of this: it was emotionally difficult to articulate it. That's why therapy is necessary—I had a session devoted to this. It will take my entire life to exorcise these demons. I know I'll have to deal with hatred directed at me—I'll have my humanity negated—until the last day of my life. It's continuous. You see it in the routine of the prisons, of the neighborhood, in how the police will constantly stop people.

When I talk about the armors, the risk is that I will find myself without them and feel even more vulnerable. Each phase of life has its own armors. As a child, I found it very difficult to maintain an armor, it seemed easier to dodge dangers. But as time goes by, you begin to confront the hatred because you know it's worse if you don't. Each confrontation adds another layer to the armor. At the same time, each new layer means another layer of isolation—you find yourself inside an ever-thicker armor, separated from other people. Emotionally, you become more and more restricted, and you become more rigid.

Because of maternity, I've been thinking often about all of these armors—and the possibilities they restrict—and how they shaped my behavior towards my son Onirê. I wish he could just skip some of the phases in which we experience the hatred, but he has to go through everything. You have to experience each phase so that you figure out how you organize yourself. It's very individual. Yet I recognize that we build a protection network inside Black families where everyone goes through the same forms of brutality—symbolic, psychological and physical—even though each person will go through them differently. Collectively we're able to forge a structure that provides greater protection.

While processing how it was to live through a context of racial brutality, racial hatred, I try to elaborate less awful ways to go through those experiences. How can you cope with this in your life, in your body, in your head? We continuously go through this: when you're in a room full of white people and you're the only Black person; when you enter college; whether on your first day at work or your fifteenth year at work, you experience the same situation. It's always about re-elaborating an African identity in the world, constantly.

João: Can you speak about the individual and collective armors? How does Rise Up provide a collective armor?

Andreia: When we're in a Rise Up activity, we meet other people; when we see a Black child, a Black woman, or Black men—we identify with each other immediately because they all look like our own families. Rise Up has been helping me unveil the monster. Because before Rise Up, I had this illusion that, eventually, antiblack hatred will not affect us, it won't find us. I understood that sometimes it's better to dodge the situation than confront it, and it guarantees that you won't put yourself in direct and immediate danger.

In a collective, the construction of that armor gives you strength to unveil the monster that's right in front of you. This is reinvigorating because otherwise you're just inside your own armor, and you're forgotten. Once you feel you belong to a group, your self-esteem is strengthened because you share a history of not being the norm. In that group of people, you feel complete belonging—physically, emotionally, socially. You can be yourself because you don't need to be constantly on alert: you belong and you are protected. That's how you reestablish your self-esteem, which goes hand-in-hand with the valuing of an identity that is denied as soon as a child begins school, if not before.

We established a school we collectively decided was an African territory. When we march as Rise Up or Die! we say, "Today no Black person dies; today the Bahia Military Police will not kill a single Black person." We know exactly who is our enemy, we know what they are capable of, and we are collectively unveiling the enemy while we are protecting each other. All of these actions have enabled our own protection while facing the monster head on and calling him out. That's how we moved beyond this notion that racism can somehow be rendered less lethal, less brutal, less impactful; we reject the hope that hatred against us can be lessened if only we dress properly, behave properly, use our hair properly. Rise Up gave me strength to identify the monster and to unmask the monster. But it's not easy, it's never going to be easy.

João: Rise Up or Die! activists demonstrate high self-esteem. Their posture is quite distinct, they're forceful and confident. Can you please talk about how self-esteem is recuperated and nourished in Rise Up? It seems to me that Rise Up provides a specific vocabulary in terms of self-recognition and collective belonging.

Andreia: In this system the white world established, the person who doesn't possess the needed prerequisites doesn't belong. That excluded person is emptied of any form of power and any form of existence as a fellow human being. When I was called a monkey, or Michael Jackson, or any of the many demeaning terms we who have dark skin are familiar with, what was articulated was that I simply didn't belong in their world. When you're called a monkey, you're emptied of any humanity and rendered an animal that is captured and put in a zoo, you're seen as not having intelligence. This, of course, is based on a history of science and theories of evolution that place Black people closer to apes. White power continuously empties us of humanity.

When we speak of self-esteem, we mean the possibility of feeling attractive and wanted, of feeling human. Inside Rise Up or Die! we reject the dominant power system and present another value system. The white world established a system that values light skin, straight hair, light eyes, and from them generated a scale of belonging. In Rise Up, we started to build our own system. We of course draw from the serious and engaged sectors of the Black movement that established an alternative value system in which Black people are centered, and which centers Africa in order to make sense of the rest of the world. It's important to understand that everything starts in the African continent, which offered the world a value system that has been neglected and vilified. From the beginning, Rise Up has encouraged the study of the African civilization in its multiple facets.

As Professor Jairo Pereira said when he saw the Winnie Mandela school: We need to re-ontologize our history because we know ourselves only through a value system that is rooted in violence against the African continent. We need to affirm ourselves despite the white world's intent to destroy us. We need to tell a child how she can rise despite the millions of people who succumbed due to racial violence, European invasion, and the Middle Passage. To tell this story is a form of care. How did we organize ourselves despite such overwhelming forces? Importantly, we need to recognize these destructive forces that continue to oppress us and threaten our existence. But we persevere and we continue to build. We built a school, we now have our own publishing house, we have care networks, we have capoeira, and we have several other practices that sustain us.

We need to keep talking about our own history within our Black families. We need to do this constantly, beyond our yearly march in August in which we wear black and red, representing our skin and the blood we spilled over centuries. On that day, we say that our struggle is to ensure that no Black person will be killed. Our alternative value system builds from our collective analysis and our frontal struggle against an enemy that sometimes is invisible, an enemy that often tries to infiltrate us.

João: Hamilton mentioned a deep sadness as it relates to creative hatred. Can you please speak on this?

Andreia: I'm not sure I'd call it sadness. In Rise Up, we hail people to confront our reality, to understand it, and in the process we build a sense of collective belonging. This sense of belonging emerges from us having our feet in the mud, as it were. It's not so much about removing sadness or employing sadness. What we don't do is bring up a false happiness—there's so much collective suffering. Given that we experience collectively how the state and society neglect us, we think that even individual celebrations are difficult. I don't think it's a deep sadness; for me it's about living our difficult reality and from it, without illusions, struggling collectively and striving to guarantee our own survival. We need to always remember that, because of antiblack hatred, we cannot let our guard down, we can't get distracted with false promises, and we can't live with the illusion that we can save ourselves individually. White people can afford to have those kinds of illusions because they see themselves individually.

Our reality shows us that we are in a position of impossibility. We're constantly violated, and that's what generates our own understanding as a people and as a collective. Yet for us it's not about living this condition in a pessimistic way, or living without joy. Rather, it's about fully living this complex and hard reality and from it building something better that is connected to our mode of existing. So it's not about getting stuck in a sentiment of impossibility, but just the opposite: based on the awareness of and against everything that negates us as a people, we want to construct new possibilities.

Rise Up isn't just about critical analysis; we concretize possibilities of living according to the values in which we believe. We're in a movement that goes in the opposite direction of that which negates us. We built a school according to our principles, where Black kids learn about our history before and after leaving the African continent, and are encouraged to imagine an autonomous future based on our strength and our accumulated knowledge.

This is not about just looking at what puts us at a disadvantage, but rather at the possibilities. For example, we now have our own publishing house. It makes a difference when you can hold a book that one of us wrote and was published by us. We also have food programs, which indicate we can grow and share our own food, and we can build other communitarian gardens. These are examples of possible ways of living according to our own concepts. In doing so, we reconstruct knowledge that was violently silenced when the African continent was looted.

We often hear people criticize Rise Up or Die! activists, saying, "You're always pouting, you seem to be permanently unhappy." In reality, it's not that we're unhappy, but that we can't be happy in this current state of affairs, which is very different. When we commit in this way, we can't be happy gratuitously—we need to create our happiness. For us, happiness is constructing our own world, which is the possibility of existing according to our principles rooted in African perspectives. This is an endless task. We're not seeking integration, which often is conflated with happiness. Integration means whiteness, or proximity to whiteness, which allows access to spaces of privilege, to consumer goods, and to sentiments like happiness. Rather than seeking someone else's project, we have our own project. According to some people, we're unhappy. Quite the opposite: we're very happy because we have our own project.

João: Can you speak about the emphasis Rise Up puts on dark-skinned people? It seems like an important reflection given the common hesitation in bringing up this theme, as if it could drive Black people away from each other. How does this emphasis on dark-skinned Black people relate to the vision of Rise Up?

Andreia: The Black person who moves in the world with dark skin is read very differently than the one who is light-skinned. I'm read as a reflection of the African history, as a history that was interrupted and was attacked. When I move in the world, I'm read as evidence that the project to eliminate Africa was not successful—of course, I represent a collective presence. At the same time, for me it's an extremely violent experience. I move in a world that associates dark skin, a large nose, and Black-textured hair with a series of negative ingrained personality traits. It's very different how the world reads a person who identifies as Black but has light skin—this violence does not affect light-skinned people the same way. In Brazil we frequently hear a white person addressing a light-skinned person who identifies as Black by saying, "You're not that Black." For me, this means the person is not so African, and doesn't carry as much of the history of Africa as other dark-skinned people whose African-ness is undeniable. The light-skinned person is closer to power, to privilege, to wealth, to beauty standards. Regardless of where I find myself—Brazil, North America, South America, Europe—I'm impacted directly and unambiguously, regardless of my occupation as a doctor. That's why Rise Up is an organization where dark-skinned people are engaged in a restructuring project.

The majority of people who are in Rise Up are dark-skinned, so those who come already have this understanding. Our role models are mostly dark-skinned Black people. We also look at the numbers and analyses on race, including those relative to the prison system, violent deaths, and the spaces of power. We do this all the time, especially during elections when the political parties say they want to include Black people. We also discuss the relationship between occupational status and skin tone: the lighter the person's skin, the higher the occupational status will be, and inversely, the darker the skin, the lower the occupational status.

It's undeniable that desire, and one's subjectivity, are impacted by this beauty standard that valorizes whiteness and degrades blackness. This is part of our unconscious, something we learn as children—what is beautiful and what is not beautiful. We're all deeply formatted by those ideas. Beauty standards are linked to power—who has access to what resources. We need to discuss our strategies all the time. From the perspective of an individual project, having a lighter-skinned child may seem like a way to protect that child from the worst kind of antiblack discrimination. But this strategy also reveals a great distance from a collective project.

We're not going to impose rules on affective relationships, on whom one should love and with whom one will have children. But we want to focus all our energy and our possibilities on who believes we have a specific collective manner of being, and that the construction of our object of desire is also collective. It's a two-way street: the collective consciousness comes from an individual consciousness, which in turn is impacted by how we collectively construct ourselves. If, as a collective, we understand that our individual being is necessarily part of the larger group, then we're asserting the possibility that we'll be able to support and reinforce those who look like us.

People who seek integration, and believe in integration as a path for them, are reading another type of possibility beyond the violence one experiences for having dark skin. In Bahia there's the expression "to lighten up the belly" (*clarear a barriga*), which is a strategy of avoiding all that violence. But this strategy does not guarantee that all will work out. It's not what we're seeking; we're seeking reaffirmation as belonging to an African people with dark skin.

To have lighter-skinned children, or even white children, is to reinforce a project of elimination. It aligns with what eighteenth- and nineteenth-century eugenicists predicted would happen in Brazil: that it would become a nation of miscegenated and white people in which Africans would be eliminated. Our presence proves the project failed, but it requires constant employment of survival strategies. One of those strategies is to guarantee that we can live our lives to the fullest and have access to what we need, including Black love as a possibility for constructing our existence and permanence. It's not an easy task, especially for younger people who carry in them the notion of a mixed world that is beautiful and integrated. Unfortunately, that notion comes with the unawareness of the erasure of blackness and its accompanying forms of violence that integration necessitates. When the possibility of loving a dark-skinned person is negated, the possibility of a Black collective is also negated. When we can't see a dark-skinned person as someone with whom we can construct a project of love, we are helping our own elimination. The white discourse, by stressing that we're all equal, constantly attacks this possibility of Black love. We know we're not all equal, and we don't want to be equal. We want to love Black people; we should love Black people as much as we should love ourselves.

BLACK TRANSNATIONAL LOVE

João: We started talking about deep sadness and we arrived at Black love.

Andreia: We always say that we want to direct our energy to our possibilities, not the impossibilities; so it's much more about Black love than sadness; it's more about the possibilities of affection than the fact that they are constantly attacked and violated.

João: What is your take on Black love? How does it relate to the Black struggle?

Andreia: We learned about the concept of love in Pan-Africanism, and we learned our concept of love in the practice. Black love is what propels us to do all that we do. It's the energy that moves people to restructure our lives. It's this love that allows me to recognize myself in someone that looks like me, and in the process I create connections that are necessary in the labor of collective reconstruction. This is Black love. It's in all that we do. It's in the love between women, between men, between trans people, between women and men. It's this love that drives us to dedicate our time to building a life project in which we need to teach children, in which we need to hail young people, in which we need to listen to the elder, and in which we need to go to the less visible and most destitute spaces.

This Black love is so vast and profound, it's immeasurable. It's not exactly romantic love, but it is also romantic love. In the last seventeen years, this Black love made it so that Rise Up or Die! persisted and reinvented itself, sought new strategies, and retreated when necessary. Rise Up provides coherence to what we understand is a life project.

At times there's some confusion. People think Black love will forgive everything, when in fact it makes it possible for us to be critical of each other and of others. Black love compels us to seek our communities, and to seriously engage experiences and knowledges that are usually disregarded. Black love and Black struggle inspire us to keep on going. I can identify with any Black person in the world, and I can understand and feel their experiences. Black love, in its vastness, is what links us despite the geographical distance that separates us. I can empathize with the suffering of Black people in countries like Mozambique, Spain, South Africa, and the United States. Black love has a lot to do with what put us in the world in the first place; it's what keeps us connected despite the forced separation, and Black love goes back to an ancestrality we all share. I'm not sure if I can explain it like this, in words. It's not about a superficial love, it's a sentiment that puts us in a condition of mutual belonging, and it allows us to be permanently mobilized.

Recently, I had the opportunity to go to Portugal, Spain, and France. In Portugal, I met a family from Cape Verde. They weren't recognized as Portuguese by the Portuguese, they were treated like African immigrants. They had been born in Portugal, they had formal citizenship. I felt as much as a foreigner when I had conversations with African women who live in Portugal, Spain, and France as when I'm in Brazil. When I arrived in France, I was questioned several times at the airport; I was asked what I was doing there, what was my profession, who I was with. They looked at my passport several times. They were trying to understand my body's presence in that space, they don't go together. It's quite complex, and at the same time it has to do with the continuity of our territory's violation, which is represented by our Black bodies. When I travel the world, I'm the African territory traveling the world. Regardless of where I am. When an airline company attendant tells me I'm in the wrong line—as it happened in Brazil—there's so much going on. She didn't ask, she affirmed. It's the same phenomenon when a white patient sees me in my white coat with my name on it, and she asks when is the doctor going to see her.

In Europe, the question I heard most often was, "Where are you from?" I'd say Brazil, and people would ask again, "But where are you from originally?" Because of my dark skin, people don't have any doubt I'm African. Because I refuse to do a DNA test and was born in Rio Grande do Sul, there's an even greater difficulty in finding out about my ancestry. I may not know exactly where in Africa I came from, but I'm certainly recognized as an African woman.

The questions from African people in Europe reiterated that I have no place—they pointed out that I had no specific belonging. All of this is extremely violent: I'm not from Brazil; I don't belong in Brazil; I was brought to Brazil via my ancestors whose origins I don't know; therefore, I have nowhere to call home.

Every time I'm called a monkey, every time I witness brutality against another Black person, especially by the police and the prison system, and also against women in the health care system; every time I'm disrespected at a police station when I'm trying to file a report: it's part of living in a violent territory in which we don't belong.

For me it's a continuum; ever since we were removed from the African continent and spread throughout the world, we're read as if we're out of place, everywhere. Leaving Brazil makes this more evident: there's a continuity regarding the negation of our humanity and our civilization practices. We're told that we don't belong anywhere, even in the territory from which we were taken. There's a continuity in the forms of oppression. Both the violence and the responses to that violence, there's a continuum throughout the world. It's related to what we call sequela. Even though slavery ended, its effects continue. They push us, scare us, and keep us closed off from each other.

When we meet other Black people in Portugal, the US, Cuba, Argentina, Uruguay—we recognize each other. Even though there are specificities to each place, we recognize each other's struggles, and we learn from each other. We've been struggling ever since leaving Africa. We learn from Winnie Mandela, for example, who struggled until her eighties, experiencing torture and incarceration. Her experience helps us to imagine how we can organize. Winnie helped feed people—she formed people. She elaborated important theories based on her everyday practice, which is something Rise Up cherishes. Our theories don't come from outsiders, but from our quotidian struggle. Unfortunately, this type of theory is not validated. We study other Black people's trajectories, their choices, their concepts, and the possibilities they open up.

With the Sequestro publishing house we published Assata Shakur's autobiography; we made it accessible to those without the means to acquire a book. Shakur describes the same situations I faced growing up. Recently, I saw an interview with Viola

Davis in which she said that, when school was over, she would run back home to evade the white boys who attacked her and called her a monkey. No one understood why she'd run home. Shakur describes experiences similar to Davis's and mine; and the children at our Winnie Mandela school relate analogous experiences when they go to white neighborhoods in Salvador. Hence the experience of continuity. Our Black collective experience is important both in terms of the similarities that bind us, and also the strategies of survival and resistance.

Like the Black Panthers, we consider society's institutions insufficient, so we need to have breakfast programs, we need to feed the children; we have many Black people with sickle cell-related conditions, we need services that care for people with that condition. Beyond the marches and rallies, and beyond the programs already in place, Rise Up or Die! considers it to be urgent to build shelters for Black people victimized by police brutality and who have to leave their homes; people who are food insecure; who have no formal education; and who have no social structures of support.

João: You mentioned various influences in different parts of the world. Could you please talk about the difference in your approach vis-a-vis that of US organizations with which you're familiar?

Andreia: We have our specificities here in Brazil. In the US, there's a memory of lynchings, which is very present. In Brazil, we're still under the myth of integration, of racial democracy, as if we're all Brazilian. The memory of slavery, and the fact that since abolition we've been pushed to the worst places and conditions, have enabled our own recognition as Black people. Sometimes we evoke names like Oscar Grant and Sandra Bland as examples of people who wanted to realize their dreams in a country with supposedly many opportunities. But because of the same mark we carry, their lives were taken as part a white supremacist project. In the US and Brazil you have two white supremacy projects that, in their own specific ways, while claiming to be in favor of integration, don't allow for it to take place. While claiming there's racial democracy, these two projects kill and exclude Black people.

In Brazil, Black people are numerically and proportionately greater than in the US; we're the majority. Yet we don't occupy spaces of power. That's why we bring up death as one of the objective elements with which to understand how white supremacy brings our elimination via public policies, police brutality, medical negligence and malpractice. On the one hand there's a narrative that stresses race mixture, and on the other, there's the continued premature death of Black people. In the US there's the emergence of certain Black institutions after emancipation, which signaled a parallel process without integration.

Rise Up or Die! doesn't promote integration. We say that we're a people, we have our own history and trajectory, we have our own way of looking at the world, we have a perspective on life and death, and we look at our existence in our own manner. Integration does not fulfill our project. When we talk about premature death, we take into account that, when a young Black person is killed, there's a series of diseases that are triggered in his family and community. For example, his mother may develop depression that leads to her death. It's difficult to establish a causal nexus, but the death of young Black men is an objective datum of our elimination. The overwhelming majority of homicides in the state of Bahia is of young Black men; and in 2020 in Salvador, all those killed by the police were Black.[6]

I have a sense that, culturally, Black people in the US feel they're American. In Brazil there's something similar when people say, for example, "We want to blacken the university." But they want to be part of an institution, and even a country, in which they'll never be accepted. In Rise Up we understand we're not part of the country. We don't feel Brazilian because this country doesn't want us. The Black Panther project resonated with us because they recognized they needed a parallel project.

I'm soon going to be fifty-one years old, and I don't expect any of this will change in my lifetime. Of course, when we think about Aretha Franklin singing for Michelle and Barack Obama in the White House, that is quite significant, especially when we contrast it to Billy Holiday singing "Strange Fruit" at a time when the prospect of a Black president was nonexistent. For some US Black groups, integration is a viable route. I don't think it has any effect on our vulnerability and death. It's wonderful to have Aretha singing in such spaces, but it is far from symbolizing any kind of power. Obama had Shakur placed at the top of a most-wanted terrorist list. Can we say the presence of a Black person in a position of power in Brazil will guarantee food, or a nonviolent police?

COMANDO VITAL

João: Can you talk about the Comando Vital?

Andreia: In Rise Up or Die! we constantly discuss, revisit, revise, resignify, and perfect our concepts. We draw from social theory, and we draw from our own practice. One of our central concepts is the Comando Vital (Vital Command), or Força Vital (Vital Force). It emerged from the recognition that we, Black women, are the vitality of our community, of our people, insofar as we are the ones who dare to give birth, and we understand the necessity of our continuity. We're the ones who nurse, care, treat, and prevent disease. Studies show that relative to nonblack women, we have a greater probability of losing our children before they are five years old, but this is our reality due to a lack of access to adequate care and the brutality under which Black families live. But, overall, our children make it to adolescence and adulthood. Women also provide financial resources via entrepreneurship and informal work in areas such as domestic work, beauty and care, health, preparing and selling food, laundry—Black women guarantee their families' livelihood. Black women are dying more frequently, they're incarcerated at increasing rates, which is a reality similar to the US.

It's women who are in the lines outside the prisons—often sleeping overnight in those lines—to bring food and support for other women and men. They travel long distances, and they endure the demeaning and brutal intimate searches. It's women who go to the Coroner's Office to recognize the bodies of their children and loved ones victimized by deadly violence, often by the state. It's Black women who put their bodies in front of the police guns. It's Black women who are at the marches and rallies—we have similar images of this all over the world, just like in South Africa, when the men were arrested or dead. It's Black women who strive to keep their families together despite such overwhelming brutality.

Our Força Vital is Black women's power to guarantee the survival of our communities. We recognize that Black women's central presence in our communities represent the Comando Vital for Black people.

Hamilton: The women's command and the women's presence, both actual and ancestral, are central to everything we do. We've been able to survive and maintain our humanity because of an African cosmovision in which women have the power—it's a matri-potency (*matripotência*). At no moment did the women abandon the struggle; rather, they articulated the struggle, which means not only did they articulated the strategy, not only did they poison the masters and plot against them, but they also took up arms and commanded armies, like Zeferina here in Pirajá with several other women. The rich history of revolts in Bahia have women at the command. But women are also spiritually nourishing their communities, reaffirming their belonging. Our communities survive and maintain themselves because women are in charge, sustaining their families, taking the streets, and providing support at the prisons.

There will be a leap when our communities recognize women's vital command. But we're cautious. Our analysis suggests it will take more than sixty years to build a successful movement. In Rise Up or Die! we had an initial spark articulating people— even though we were severely criticized by academics, Marxists, Pan-Africanists, each defending their theories. We also produced theory, but within our reality, living our lives. We wanted more than just analysis—we wanted to change society and reality itself.

SEQUELA

João: Can you talk about the concept of sequela? It seems like it's a tool for both analysis and for social change.

Andreia: The concept of sequela draws from processes that have ended but which generate ongoing consequences. Even though slavery formally ended, its consequences rebuild themselves as if it never ended. There's the negation of humanity, of life possibilities, there's the physical assassination—the elimination of absurd numbers of people with African markers—all this continuously reenacts the invasion of Africa on my body and on the bodies of Black people.

Even though it's difficult to pinpoint a specific moment or fact that defines sequela, I think of my mother's experience, at twelve, of working in a white family's house where all her needs were neglected because she was a Black girl—all this would be unimaginable for a white girl. My mother signified Africa, her body represented the African territory: this is the most defining fact. Based on this perspective, I can say that slavery in the cotton and sugar fields extends to our present. It continues, and I routinely experience its sequelae. For example, when my son leaves the house to go to the store, if he takes longer than a certain amount of time, I relive brutality, invasion, and the negation of humanity. I constantly live this negation that my mother, her mother, her grandmother, her great-grandmother and other families also certainly went through.

While there's an ongoing discussion about the definition of trauma, I think the concept is insufficient to account for all these processes because we live them as if there's no temporal lapse; it's as if I'm still living slavery. Two months ago, I was coming into the apartment building where I live; a white woman who also lives in it asked me in which apartment I worked [as a domestic servant]. What is this if not the continuation of the violent invasion of our territory in the African continent? So we're not talking about one fact, but a whole set of facts.

The concept of sequela helps us understand and organize given the context of Black genocide. I'm obviously influenced by a Western medical formation, but I know I must go beyond it if I'm to grasp our specific reality. For example, in the field of biomedical health, when someone has a stroke, or a vascular encephalic accident, sometimes the person has a sequela after the cause is no longer. They will have difficulty in walking, talking, they'll feel tingling; there are various technical terms.

In the context of slavery, even though it formally ended in Brazil in 1888, we continue to experience its sequela, as if the cause is constantly remade. Our bodies are still treated as if slavery is present, and we continue to experience myriad consequences. Our disproportionate presence in the carceral system, our daily brutalization in the streets, our monitoring in stores, our out-of-placeness in spaces of privilege, the denial of our humanity: it's as if we constantly relive slavery. The concept of sequela allows us to grasp the meaning of our presence in the wake of our kidnapping out of the African continent. It's not like stress after a traumatic event, but rather the constant and daily remaking of enslavement as it is experienced on our bodies. The concept allows us to reflect on our political and structural predicament as one of slavery.

João: Could you provide an example of sequela?

Andreia: The criminal justice system's modi operandi are the greatest examples of how we still live slavery today. Black people are always the main suspects: those involved in illicit activities, they presumably have the same African traits I have. It's always Black or Brown people (*pessoas pardas*) who have Black-textured hair, who walk a certain way, who have dark skin. A recent example is of a judge in the state of Paraná, Inês Marchalek Zarpelon, who in 2020 condemned a forty-eight-year old man to fourteen years of prison citing in her sentence the fact that his criminal behavior was "due to his race."[7] If we do a quick newspaper search, we'll see that Black people are often killed when they're mistaken for an alleged criminal. There's a case of a young Black dentist who was about to get into his imported car when he was shot in the head. There had been a robbery nearby, and the suspect was described as a Black man, which prompted the police to go after every Black man, culminating with this execution. Another recent case was in a condominium in Rio, where a Navy agent shot and killed a Black man who lived there. The Navy agent, a white man, thought the Black man was there to rob the building.

Our criminal justice system is just like our society. Both have the Black person as their standard enemy. It's no surprise that when we look into the Brazilian prisons, Black women and men are disproportionately represented. Slavery, so-called scientific racism as propagated by Lombroso, Garofalo, and Nina Rodriguez in Brazil, solidified the association between certain African physical traits to criminal behavior.[8] Moreover, those theories suggested a racial hierarchy in which Black people were seen as unfit to be self-determining and therefore unfit to live in society. These theories still reverberate loudly in society and in the criminal justice system in particular.

João: As a medical doctor, can you talk about the ways in which the concept of sequela manifests itself in patterns of collective health and how disease can be linked to the afterlife of slavery?

Andreia: From the perspective of public health, studies from the US, not yet published in Brazil, show when there's racial alignment in high-risk childbirth, there's a greater chance of the child's survival. In other words, when a Black family is treated by Black health professionals, the outcomes are markedly better. White doctors sometimes believe that Black patients are less intelligent and won't understand their instructions and will be more susceptible to abuse prescriptions as well as illicit drugs.

From the perspective of medical practice, in Brazil we have studies that show Black women receive less anesthesia during childbirth because doctors believe Black women feel less pain than white women. Black women's consultations are systematically shorter than white women's, and also during gynecological exams doctors touch Black women less frequently than they touch white women. This reflects the behavior of medical practitioners. We don't have a current census of the medical profession, the last one was published in 2020. We know there's an increasing number of women, but from a racial perspective, we don't know how many Black doctors there are. We know doctors are influential in their medical teams. When we consider the medical profession's biased gaze towards Black people, we begin to grasp Black's people accentuated vulnerability, including the onset of sequalae.

There are many conditions that affect Black people in particular, and they are determined by racism. I mentioned what happens during labor, and how decisions regarding the type of care provided in this very delicate moment will certainly determine outcomes. We still don't have an adequate approach to illicit drug use. We still don't have an adequate understanding and much less an effective medical approach to the ways in which young Black people's development is affected by police brutality; and to how Black men's chances of being incarcerated—three times higher than white men's—affects their overall health. These common factors impact health and illness, but medicine still doesn't recognize the ways in which the many facets of racism determine one's susceptibility to illness.

If we take into account that enslaved people were overworked and died prematurely, today this is reflected in the lower life expectancy of Black people compared to whites. What we have here is the realization of different expectations regarding how long and how well one lives depending on their race.

João: Black neighborhoods usually have the worst infrastructure. The water is polluted, the air has more toxins. How are those related to premature death and to the concept of sequela? When you mention the criminal justice system, it seems to be part of this constellation of conditions within which Black people find themselves. Can you talk about how Rise Up conceptualizes these conditions, beyond the criminal justice system, and how it attempts to provide an answer to such conditions? Am I hearing correctly that your concept of sequela is applied both in the social diagnosis and in elaborating and carrying out actual interventions?

Also, these questions seem to be related to the issue of autonomy. That is, faced with such reality that the concept of sequela allows us to grasp, it becomes imperative to carry out a series of actions based on local autonomy, which would allow a better and longer life for Black people. Is this what you are saying?

Andreia: Yes. This concept allows us to grasp the consequences of our compartmentalization, of who we are, following our removal from Africa. It's difficult for us to see ourselves as part of a collective and integrated into nature. We try to reconnect ourselves with an African humanity in an integral manner. This is far more complete and complex than what the West can understand. It's not an easy task. We're trying to relearn. But we have to be attentive to how continuous sequelae establish themselves and impact not only our health, but also our education, culture, leisure, and relationship to others.

It's only when we undertake the exercise to look at ourselves with all this complexity that we begin to understand. Health, for us, is equal to life, and our life has all these facets that are inseparable: my health is not separate from pleasure, from reading, from fun, from my connection to nature. My health requires that I have access to water, food, information—I need the codes with which to read the world. To access all of this, we need to reintegrate. Health is not just the absence of all that brings disease—when the police doesn't stop me, when they don't brutalize me, incarcerate me. But health and well-being mean having all the necessary social and spiritual connections so that I can have my needs met. The connection with the planet is essential.

This is how we re-ontologize ourselves. The sequelae are constantly remaking themselves, but that's why we need a broad program of reconstruction, that's why we need a school, and institutions that can retell our history, where we are the majority and we're self-determined. That's why we need to study those who helped us get back on our feet—Zeferina, Mandela, Malcolm, Assata—the people who helped us get here. We need to relearn. To have a community garden is to relearn how to live integrally. We need to produce what we eat; we need to understand that the food we plant and eat gives us agency. We need to learn how to produce food because what the world is showing is that we have increasingly less access to things we depend on. During the pandemic, we had to undertake food gathering campaigns: we found ourselves having to take food inside the prisons, where people were supposedly under the care of the state. But the state is killing us, it will not provide food or water, and it's telling us that we need to fend for ourselves. In the prisons, we anticipated this crisis. Prisons literally deprive people of water for two or three days. In our neighborhoods, we're also vulnerable. That's why we need to relearn how to produce our own food and obtain our own water. We're getting sick from preventable causes more often and earlier in our lives.

All this is interconnected. When we're speaking about our lives, we're talking about health, disease, the production of food. We need to figure out our roles in our communities. We need doctors, lawyers, people who know how to find and treat water, transform trash into fertilizer, people who know how to build houses, who know how to plant trees. We need to become a collective again, one that is able to generate what we need—that's our project. That's why we're reaching out, that's how we're going to build possibilities, and for that we need to bring knowledge back into our Black communities. It's very complex. So you want to be a lawyer? Excellent, because we know at some point this knowledge will be important for our community. But regardless of what you study and become an expert in, you need to dialogue with our community, and with what's going on here. If you're a doctor and you're not willing to do that, it's of no use; you need to dialogue with local knowledge about medicinal plants. There are ancient practices that can be useful, like acupuncture or auriculotherapy.

For us there's no temporal break between slavery and what we experience today. We're trying to reconstitute who we were before leaving Africa: integral beings, complex beings, and collective beings. Individuality works for whites; it doesn't work for us. We're collective beings, but we have been separated from that understanding. To have children, for me, means continuity, resistance; not as an empty concept, but as a practice based on a comprehension that we don't want to disappear from this world. As the original people, Black Africans have the responsibility to guarantee our continuity. So to have children goes beyond an individual perspective, it means opposing the processes of elimination that impact us. Black love cements the collective project.

João: I'm hearing you lay out a project of affirmation that is at the same time a project of refusal. The affirmation is in having Black children and in producing conditions for well-being. The refusal is in not accepting sequelae, and also refusing the electoral system, refusing the given conditions, refusing Black death. There's also refusal of mothers who, during slavery, chose to sacrifice their children rather than have them live under such conditions. The stance of refusal I see in Rise Up seems to be related, one that refuses the given conditions.

Andreia: As a dark-skinned Black mother, some movie scenes impact me strongly. In *Amistad* there's a scene when one of the enslaved people is going to be executed, and the camera moves towards a young mother carrying a child. Suddenly the mother disappears. She jumped into the ocean with her child. Imagine the first time I saw that scene; later on I became aware of similar scenes in other movies and books. They bring a lot of pain. We were able to make it to this point because many women decided to sacrifice themselves and their children. This to me is Black love, which relates to how mothers put their bodies in front of police officers when the state comes to brutalize our communities. Their lives can easily be taken away. We need to remember all such acts. The woman who jumped into the ocean refused to integrate, she refused to submit to the white man's rules and wishes. We need to remember and learn from all of this. All that my mother, grandmother, great-grandmother, great-grandfather did—it was because of what they sacrificed that I got here.

It's from understanding the cost of what all our ancestors did that we refuse the electoral system that wants to integrate a few Blacks. Our refusal continues the refusal that was carried out so that our people were not subjected. The quilombolas represent a political refusal: they expressed Black people's power to organize autonomously and not submit to the regime and to integration. They understood that it was necessary to organize, resist, battle and kill white people when needed. We define ourselves as a continuity of the quilombo. The quilombolas did not elaborate their worldview inside the master's house; they weren't hanging out with whites; they organized autonomously. That's why we often say, "Quilombos don't ask permission, quilombos don't beg. Quilombos take." Our collective project is not serving a party, it's not serving a particular group. It is ours, for our emancipation, for our rising, and for our continuity. Refusal is one of the fundamental elements for our continuity as a people. Individual success will never be more important than the Black collective struggle.

CHAPTER FOUR
FUTURITY

In this concluding chapter, taking into account their seventeen years as Rise Up's central organizers, Andreia and Hamilton reflect on their visions of the future.

QUILOMBISMO

João: You mentioned Quilombismo during our conversations and suggested Rise Up or Die! has its own version of it.

Hamilton: Abdias do Nascimento was the first to talk about this, and wrote about it. He made wonderful and fundamental contributions. I don't like theoretical fraud, so we always cite the sources.[1] I also admire Beatriz Nascimento, and her vision of the quilombo was consistent with her practice.[2]

In Rise Up we took both thinkers into account, and formulated our own perspective. We say that quilombolas don't ask. The insight emerged when we were in front of the governor's office protesting a police killing of a Black youth. A group of Workers' Party members were there too. The police arrived, and the Workers' Party folks fled. That's when we entered the building. We've always told the police, "If you're going to beat us up or kill us, go right ahead." We learned that from Steve Biko, who also said that the less you collaborate with the police, the less they'll beat you up. We haven't been beaten up, but we've been killed. We've always had the strategy of not asking for anything.

When we looked at Abdias's life, we noticed that the organizations in which he belonged or founded always asked for this or that. Quilombolas, on the other hand, don't ask. We understand that we're always immersed in violence.

We're in relative peace now, but that's because we decided to take a step back. They just killed ten kids the other day, and we didn't say anything. We've been doing reflection activities, men's circles, activities with women. This is similar to Beatriz do Nascimento's notion of quilombola peace. There's a lot of resistance against what we say, that's why I'm seldom called to give talks at certain places. But I still give many talks, and I often say the quilombolas leave a trail of blood wherever they go; they decapitate the enemy's heads, they bury children alive. The quilombolas don't ask for freedom, they don't ask for a plot of land, they don't beg for food or for clothes. The quilombolas burn the plantation. If you're not willing to burn the plantation, then you're not a quilombola.

If there's a conceptual mistake here, it's not Abdias's, it's not Beatriz's, it's ours. It's based on our experience of seeing people decapitated, shot, incarcerated, sick, depressed, frustrated, anxious. Our lives are really heavy.

We gave Quilombismo a new meaning because we don't believe in integration, which was central in how Abdias do Nascimento thought about it. We have no optimism regarding integration.

We also stress that autonomy and freedom are not to be asked for; we build them with our own hands. We don't believe in Brazil. We don't want anything from Brazil; we just want to open a space in this territory and create zones of freedom. That's Quilombismo for us.

Differently than Abdias do Nascimento, we don't want to dispute the state, we don't believe in this democracy, and we don't believe in interracial relations, be they political or affective. It's been demonstrated by those who came before us, these concepts are weak and harm us. We believe that we create our own state, or we create pieces of a state, and that is a fundamental concept for us.

João: Would you say that your version of Quilombismo is an attempt to recuperate the stolen possibilities?

Hamilton: Our vision of Quilombismo is to concretely revitalize Black revolt. When Zeferina led a slave revolt against General Labatut, the motto was, "Long live the Black, death to the white!" That's the Quilombismo I practice. It's not about antiracist education. Black writers aren't read, and they don't become part of the basic educational curriculum. That's because both the left and the right despise us. Instead of creating our own institutions and structures, and circulating our own books, we keep waiting, or asking the white government and society to be benevolent towards us, it's a peaceful attitude. But only a frontal war will bring change. In Rise Up or Die! we've always talked about weapons and getting ready by learning and training. The radical right distributed weapons widely and they'll start shooting Black people, linking us to Workers' Party people, who they also hate. Just having dreadlocks, like me, will be enough for them to think

I'm a communist. But in my case, my reaction will be quite different, if you know what I mean.

João: Quilombismo then is preparation for war. Please tell me how you understand this war. How will it take place?

Hamilton: We need to get ready. We're not going to initiate it because we don't have the conditions to sustain it. We don't have the financial, psychological, or structural means to carry it out. MNU also thought about war at some point. In the last fifteen years, we lost sixty years, which means we have at least another sixty years to get ready. Some so-called Black intellectuals are now doing ads for expensive alcoholic drinks while we're busting ourselves to get people together for a Saturday morning gathering. We address people who drink, who waste the money that was set aside for school supplies or for food; we tell the person alcohol is destroying their life.

We can't carry out a war. We're not psychologically prepared. We're preparing to live in peace, but if we're attacked, we'll respond in kind. We need to have our own land and defend it; we need to create the conditions in which the police don't have access. But it won't happen anytime soon. Right now, we have armed brothers who won't hesitate to shoot at us. That's why I say it will take sixty years. Our task now is to prepare the terrain. We have this building, the Winnie Mandela School; now we need to get land where we can plant and have our own wells. All of this is in the book I wrote, a book that is imagining a future.[3]

João: So this is a moment of self-defense.

Hamilton: Self-defense means we have to stay in our territory; we have to stop petty crime, stop drinking, stop doing drugs. We need to study and train our body. What are we going to do? Kidnap the US ambassador? Take over the buses and trains? What is there to gain? We do need to defend ourselves; we need a team of lawyers to help us free people from prison, we need the resources for that. That person who is freed will ideally join the struggle. Zeferina didn't go to war because she provoked the war; she went to war because they attacked her and her people, who cultivated the land, they were self-sustained, and many people fled slavery to join them. A special police battalion was created to deal with her. She didn't provoke anything. And she didn't negotiate because she knew it would be useless.

João: Can you elaborate on self-defense and how it became central for Rise Up?

Hamilton: We tried everything. In the past, we tried having a voice in the parliament by supporting Black elected officials so they could amplify our voice. We did that at the municipal, state, and federal levels. We found out that our parliamentary adventure was a mirage because it's all coordinated by whites, on the left and on the right. To survive in those spaces, Black representatives have to broker deals that don't benefit us in the least, and we're left with promises or small reforms in a building—this society—that's already decrepit.

Our finding, in the real struggle (*dentro da luta real*)—in the Black spaces of conflict, in the spaces of disgrace—was that it was impossible for us to be in the parliament. Today, you have Black people in the major political parties running for office, which is different from the 1970s and 1980s, when we needed to have certain technical qualifications to occupy specific bureaucratic positions. Today we have people who actually believe in the parliamentary route. They're doctors, researchers, sociologists, lawyers, and engineers. Besides, of course, the historical politicians, like Benedita da Silva. Right now there's a transition from the Bolsonaro government to the new Lula government. There's a transition committee and Black people are not there. Black people created their own transition commission. It's as if we don't belong—an institutional ghetto was created with the mandate to think about the transition from a Black perspective. In reality, there's no transition, there's just the occupation of bureaucratic positions. There's no deep discussion of what's going on in Brazil.

At one point, we took to the streets to support and elect our candidates. Our elected officials had the obligation to support the masses that elected them. But they consistently sided with the government when it was killing Black people, was strengthening the police, and was ignoring patterns of summary executions. That's when we gave up on that route and focused on the rural struggle.

We embraced the idea that a utopian Black state can be realized in the territory where we live. That's Black power. We don't need socialism or Pan-Africanism to be in place for us to realize our dream. We have to realize the dream now. This is our model.

We began participating in encounters with the Movimento dos Trabalhadores Rurais Sem Terra (Landless Workers' Movement, MST), and now we're part of a network that includes Indigenous and Black rural workers. They expect us to link the urban with the rural struggles. That is, reach out to Black people who are crammed in cities, in favelas.

Favelas are not things to be preserved. We need to construct ample spaces so that we can breathe and have areas for healthy leisure activities. Right now, we live on top of each other. The pandemic showed how unhealthy favelas are. We're not able to take care of ourselves or protect ourselves. In 2005, I was in the commission that presented then-president Lula with a report showing the water we Black people drink has fecal matter. So favelas are not to be preserved—we have to demolish them and create alternative ways of living. And for that we need land. Whereas for influencers, self-care is about buying the right stuff, including the particular brand of clothing, we want land.

In discussions with the land activists, we learned that we can grow our own food without pesticides. We can drill wells and get pure water. In the near future, there's going to be a hydric war in Brazil. This is no science fiction—a shortage of water is going to affect everyone. It started already. We need to prepare now.

So these are our thoughts about self-defense. We will have territory, and we will have to defend it. In our ample territory, we'll have water, we'll have our own houses, we'll welcome people who're willing to plant. We'll have our own justice system. Who errs, who commits a crime or abuse, will be judged by us. It will be a popular type of justice, based on ancestral principles. We'll have to take care of our defense. Rise Up is already building this future, one small step at a time.

João: Hamilton, thinking about Rise Up's vision of the future, can you talk about the Black men's circles that you've been organizing?

Hamilton: Black men's transformation inside the political struggle is fundamental for us. We men need to change individually and collectively, and if we don't do that, our projects won't succeed. Based on my life experience, and in particular with my parents, my brothers, cousins, and people in my neighborhood, I think Black men try to see the world through the lens of white men. We end up trying to act like white men because we've been robbed of our own history. We don't see how Black women have been holding us together, in our communities, building and ultimately maintaining everything. That's not by accident. We come from a matriarchal civilization that was lost. Thinking through my Yoruba religion—my grandmother and my great-grandmother were Yoruba—women are the primordial divinities. The ancestral uterus generates everything. In the beginning, everything was water, and water is what is inside the uterus.

In my family, I saw the men disappearing—I've written poetry about it. They disappeared, they never took care of our family, they were always in the streets, they were always unemployed, they were always hustling and when they got money, they spent it partying. Then, starting with my generation, men got imprisoned on an industrial scale. Men in our community or in our family disappeared for one or two years, and we'd later find out they had been arrested.

In our men's circles, we talk about masculinity from our own experiences, that's how we start. We start with our own pain. We discuss the norms of masculinity we internalized and how they often translate into physical and sexual violence. In our circles, we learn that we really didn't learn how to have sex when we were sixteen; we learned it all wrong in how we are supposed to treat women, how we're supposed to treat our partners. The person that internalizes this type of violent masculinity is unbalanced, wants to dominate, including the political organization of which he's a part. It never works. In the 1980s, the MNU practically expelled and ridiculed all gay people. There was no space for women, who also left and created their own organizations. The MNU Women's Group, of which Luiza Bairros was a part, was like a parallel organization with its own theses; it struggled against the masculinist hegemony.

The men's circle provides a space to reflect on men's role in the world, they'll think about how they treat their partners and spouses. Some of the men are gay, some are very masculinist. We discuss sexuality, intimacy, how to raise children, and it gets to a point in which we're helping each other navigate our challenges. We offer to speak with their children—there are cases in which they haven't seen their kids in a while—or reach out to their partners or former partners. I think these kinds of things can change the world.

We can't make the same mistakes and have in our own political organization the same sexist practices and principles that inevitably lead to failure. A number of Black organizations, and Rise Up is no exception, unsurprisingly implode because of asymmetrical gender relations, despite efforts to deconstruct the masculinist discourse and practice.

In Rise Up, we have the Comando Vital, in which the women, including Andreia, are in charge. But often they want to consult with me, Hamilton. So even when we try to escape men's hegemony there's a deep cultural construct that renders men the center of power, knowledge, and command. It's not the women who have to figure this out, its men. Men have to learn how to say, "We're not part of the command."

In our marches, women are at the front—we have all-women divisions—and they're fearless. The women who lost their children in the process of genocide against Black people—the women who lose the light in their eyes—become empty. But they acquire a renewed soul when they join us and collectively confront the police and the state.

We men have so much garbage inside of us. We need to remove that trash, those traumas, our low self-esteem. For the men's groups to strengthen, they need to embrace the "real concrete," which means to embrace our real and concrete experiences, our traumas, pains, disappointments. I'm not sure if the pandemic amplified it, but now it seems that there's more talk of anxiety. There's also the question of drug use, which seems to be more intense and somehow naturalized—my sense is that there's more people taking pills, smoking weed, snorting coke.

I sense that we still don't know how to take care of ourselves. We're offering forms of professional care—therapists, psychiatrists, and social workers who can help us individually and collectively. That's how the men's groups are emotionally and spiritually strengthened, and when they do so, men can act constructively in their communities. Men should intervene in violence against women—this hatred that exists against women. Men usually are very homosocial. They go to soccer with other men, they only hang out with men, and when they encounter women, that hatred comes through.

Pan-Africanists and those who are into Afrocentrism usually accuse us of being feminists. For them it's a pejorative term. I'd like to be a Black feminist, and I'd like to have a healthy masculinity, without the pain and disease that Western society has forced on us. I want to take out the internalized trash. Since the

1990s, I'm trying to break the pattern. Heeding the MNU women's call to Black men, I raised my children, I took notes, I'm trying. I heard what they said: the experience of caring seemed to be exclusive to women; men needed to step up.

I only mention the MNU because it's the organization I know, I don't want to speak evil of it. There were very sophisticated people there. The men who traveled had PhDs, nice clothes. But their partners were never with them, they were at home raising children, they were sacrificing their own careers for the sake of their male partners.

I committed so many mistakes. But when I decided to raise my children, intuitively I tried to break the pattern. It was the first time I got a formal job, and it was the first time I had legal documentation. My kids lived in terrible conditions. From the little money I made, instead of buying myself nice shoes, I bought shoes for my two kids; it was all for the kids. I learned to eat at home, cook every day. I still think that I could have done much better raising them, I could have given more to them—to this day, they have difficulties. I look at the child I'm raising with Andreia, and I see how she has a much better perspective on care, on what our child needs. My oldest is about to be forty years old, and he's part of the Landless Movement. My daughter is an artist, an actress, and my other son is a boxer. I'm proud of them.

LAND

João: Can you talk about the ways in which the recent acquisition of land in the south of Bahia, by elite Brazilians and non-Brazilians, from Black landowners, presents a challenge to your plan? In the Ilhéus region, known for its cacao plantations, Black people had finally gotten their land titles following the Lula land reform measures; and now, less than a generation after that event, they're selling it to white people again.

Hamilton: Recently, I was in a town near Salvador called Boipeba. It's a paradisiacal island. There aren't buses that go there, you have to take a boat. I went there for a literary event. All the commercial establishments are owned by people from outside of Brazil: Italians, French, US Americans. I walked around and talked with local people, especially the youths. And in my talk at the event, I said that territory was ours, it was Black sacred territory. The Black youth then started to organize and protested in front of the municipal administration. They found out that one of the town's smaller islands had been sold to Italians. No one knew. The Public Prosecutor's office didn't know. Now we plan on future activities there, but things are tense. They want to remove the youths from the vending stands near the beach; they want to prohibit fishing and other traditional forms of ocean agriculture. This is similar to what is happening in the south of Bahia, near Ilhéus, which is historically dominated by Coronéis do Cacau (Cacao Colonels), which includes Jorge Amado's family, the well-known Bahia writer.

There's a settlement called Terra Vista, which is part of the historical MST. They're critical of the MST's submission to the Workers' Party, and Terra Vista doesn't participate in this. They created an exciting agricultural community in that same cacao area. Young people are at the forefront of the land they occupy. The leader is thirty-three years old.

My oldest son was involved in drugs, he was sick, I took care of him. After a spiritual treatment, my son found this Terra Vista. He stopped drinking, stopped using drugs. He learned how to cultivate the land, and now he's part of the MST leadership. This is a painful personal example that shows other young people can follow it. We sent four young people to Terra Vista, and some of them couldn't take it. It's hard work. You live in a tent, you wake up at 5 a.m., you work the land all day, and then start again the next day.

The struggle for land is a possible renovation route for the Black movement. But it's difficult to mobilize people. I remember in the 1980s and 1990s, and after with Rise Up or Die!, when we suggested communitarian action, a great many people responded. These days, you have to go door-to-door, you have to send emails. I still make posters, I make flyers, I leave them in the bakery, and no one comes. We say we're going to have health care in the neighborhood, that Dr. Andreia is going to give free consultations. This is the concrete real, but it's as if people aren't hearing us.

We're making the case to everyone who cares to listen that it's much better when you grow your own food, when you drink water you know where it comes from. Rural life provides more dignity than in the city. We've been talking about this possibility in our men's circles, in our sessions on literature, in our cinema nights, and in the prisons.

When we talk about and imagine life on the land, we strengthen ourselves, and I am hopeful. I'm usually pessimistic; I don't believe racism will ever end; I don't think we'll ever be a thriving society. But I am hopeful that we can have our own land and become autonomous. I'm betting on this.

In twenty years, I'll be an elder. I need to be in a safe place, and our current apartment is not a safe place. We're thinking about registering guns because the country is in a state of convulsion. No one is paying attention, but these crazy people who are blocking the freeways, they are legally permitted to carry guns.[4] It won't take much for them to go after political formations they see as socialist, communist. What are we going to do then? Call the police? It's the police who are facilitating all this.

To go back to Boipeba, we think that we can connect young Black people there with the young Black people in the cities like Salvador, and the young people in land settlements like Terra Vista. The young people in Boipeba are willing to move ahead with this connection, and so are young people here in Salvador. We're telling them that going back to the land will provide them with a better life. They may not have been born on the land, but your grandparents probably were. Even if it's just to breathe better air, get calmer. The land provides life alternatives.

When we have land, we begin to create our own state. No traditional state and no public policy will ever provide solutions to our problems. During the thirteen years of the Workers' Party government, we certainly experienced an increase in our buying power. But we saw all those improvements disappear as soon as Bolsonaro took over. For us, the debate about buying power is not enough. We need to produce and we need to do so in community.

João: How do you imagine reaching the young urban people? How do you break the resistance against living off the land?

Hamilton: We've had city-rural areas cultural communitarian exchanges, and the young people get really motivated. The young person may not move to the rural area immediately, but they will have contact with the land, they'll plant in our communitarian gardens. They may not want to live there, but they'll get acquainted with agricultural technology, they'll learn from those who live off the land, and they may create communities in the city based on that knowledge. This will create dynamic connections. You need people in the cities to help with the product distribution, you need infrastructure, you need resources. Today we have a building, but we need a larger structure to accommodate more people, to have a communitarian kitchen. We need to create small services that provide food, clothing.

The MST provides the possibilities of having your own home and land. We need to start offering concrete real things. This is our new step. After eighteen years, that's where we are going. We need a financial arm. Quilombo X fulfills that purpose. Our structure needs to be different. Over the years, we matured the idea of autonomy. We're in a new era, and we're about to test new ideas. We're investing in Rise Up, an organization that many thought wouldn't last six months. Many of the organizations that criticized us don't exist anymore. We're working on a plan to empower ourselves that involves not only the youth, but all Black people, it's all generations.

João: Can you talk about Quilombo X as a financial arm of Rise Up?

Hamilton: Our movement is going to be constructed from a solid base. We need resources. It's going to be for the next generation. I don't think Rise Up or Quilombo X are going to become large organizations. When the ANC started, for example, it was just half a dozen people running around, debating. Agostinho Neto and the MPLA (Movimento Popular para a Libertação da Angola—Popular Movement for the Liberation of Angola); MNU: all these organizations transformed themselves. These days, people still think of Rise Up as confrontational, they don't know what we're proposing. We're patient. Patience is revolutionary. We're carefully watering our gardens, and we're expanding.

FUTURISTIC ANCESTRALITY

João: You and Hamilton mentioned the ways in which the dead are always present with you. Can you speak more about how the worship of ancestors informs Rise Up?

Andreia: I think this is an important aspect of the diaspora. Where I was born, in the south of the country, we learned how to worship the ancestors in a very hidden way—it was forbidden. Until recently, the prohibition was a law and there could be no African cultural manifestation without a police authorization. It's different in Bahia. Rise Up or Die! made me revisit my relationship with ancestrality.

In my father and Hamilton's first encounter, they exchanged Yoruba ancestral information via songs. My generation didn't learn those songs. My father knew them because he was an Alabê.[5] There are several African religious traditions, but they don't separate us from each other, from nature. We're a unity. Of course there's individuality, but to live we need to be in communion with nature and with each other. My existence and continuity are only possible collectively. To worship ancestrality is to recognize this interconnectedness, and to recognize who came before us, who struggled, and who didn't give up on bringing me into this world.

It's this ancestrality that we reference when we march and say that we're ten thousand people, including the dead. Even though the people who are violently killed are not with us physically, they're part of the struggle, they're with us. We'd not exist if it were not for the relationship with those who came before us, like my father, grandfather, great grandfather, all those who were in Africa. All their sacrifices made it easier for me, and for those who came after them. We say their names. We choose to reaffirm them, and establish a continuity between them and us. This worship renders impossible that we think of ourselves individually, in isolation. Collective life means that we are responsible for our own lives and the lives of others. We impact each other. African matrix religions center this worship.

João: Hamilton, could you please talk more about the worship of ancestrality, not only as a spiritual aspect of Rise Up, but also as part of the practice that centers the presence of the dead?

Hamilton: I feel that Rise Up is the result of a spiritual determination. We didn't come up with anything new about genocide, quite the opposite. We received a legacy from the MNU and we gave it our perspective, which comes from ancestrality. The first dimension of ancestrality is that we're a people. Our struggle is not related to the fact that we're exploited workers, but to the fact that, as people, we created our own humanity. We were hunted, enslaved, but we weren't victims, we didn't submit. Everywhere we are present, there is evidence of our resistance. To have instruments with which to dialogue with our ancestors is important because it gives us access to their experience, their knowledge. In my body, there's a genetic register of those experiences that allows me to look back and not give up.

Another dimension is the exorbitant number of violent deaths over the decades, and often those deaths are mere numbers, part of our rhetoric and lament—or they're not even taken into account. You look at the history of the Black movement in the last fifty years, there's the struggle to allow us in social elevators, universities; there's a critical debate about health, women's rights, gay rights, police brutality—but there's nothing concrete against our deaths. In Brazil, there's no accumulation of knowledge about our deaths and our lives—dignified lives. We've been immersed in death: each person we buried, we didn't talk about them based on the Coroner's Office report, or based on academic studies. We were there, so we cite their names, we remember them as people, not as numbers: Evangivaldo, Negro Blul, Alan do Rap. I spent more than a decade of my life burying people, now I'm gardening. But it's the same thing.

We're instruments of an ancestral Yoruba legacy, which is the devolution of the physical body to earth, which is another Orixá. When someone is killed, we have a procession with the person's body throughout the city. We politicize the dead body which, until then, didn't have a political value, didn't have a symbolic value, it was only yet another dead body which no one knew about.

If we were to rationalize, we'd conclude that we didn't have the conditions to undertake any of those processions and protests. We were in no condition to confront the Military Police, the state government, the Workers' Party federal government, the extermination groups. Who knows what deflected the bullets away from us. The people for whom we had processions were not family members, they weren't anyone we knew, but they belonged to our world and were part of our people, so we thought it was our obligation to provide them a dignified burial.

In these close encounters with death, we noticed phenomena that researchers missed. The mother who lost her son and acquired an empty gaze, she was the family's breadwinner. She ended up losing her employment as a domestic worker because she was interviewed on the TV news and her boss fired her. What did we do? Rise Up gave her basic needs, we helped with the purchase of a dignified coffin for her young son. Otherwise, the body is buried in a shallow grave, and if there's a need to exhume the body for further investigation, it's a disaster.

We knew none of this, of course—we learned because we were there. The cemeteries were not part of the Black movement's itinerary, except to honor their militants. The militants that died usually had good burials, they came from relatively well-off backgrounds, and we'd all go there to pay our respects.

Based on a Yoruba perspective that is very strong in Salvador, and indeed in Brazil, we developed our vision of the world: Women are the primordial uterus, they create everything and they maintain the order. Exu is gold, and he stays at the crossroad waiting for the human in front of the uterus. The vagina, Ya Amapô, Mother Vagina, is an entity that's worshiped. And you have the earth, who has a pact with Obatalá, Ogun, Olugama, and Ajalané. The deities make the body, but they need the raw material, which earth lends to them but asks that it be returned. The raw material is returned when someone dies. Death is an Orixá, but death only charges what was borrowed when someone has fulfilled what they promised they'd accomplish while they were on earth, usually when someone is an elder. But death via violence and genocide interrupts the process. When that happens, we die two times.

In Rise Up, we debate all of this. If we come from earth and someone dies out of the natural order, you end up dying twice, and this last death is worse because, if you don't adequately return to earth—if you've been disappeared because of your politics, if you have your head cut off, if your organs are removed—you're not accepted in the realm of the dead. For a Christian, that would be an inferno.

There's no doubt that it was our capacity to dialogue with the visible and the invisible that enabled our strength and our growth, that allowed us to enter spaces we weren't supposed to enter. Obatala made my body when he blew life into it, and he sent me to earth, where I whispered in Exu's ear my goals in life. One of my original goals was to create Rise Up or Die! and create the structures that are here already. Now, imagine if I die when the cops are after me or when I'm seventeen? My existence in the universe would be completely erased.

When we speak with young people, we help reconstitute their memory, and in the process they reconstitute themselves spiritually. That's when they commit to another type of life. I'm not being symbolic or poetic. It's something in which I truly believe. I believe that a lot of things happened inside the prison when I was incarcerated; police officers shot at me several times, point blank; cops going after Andreia; our home invaded by the police. We didn't have any kind of protection, nothing. All we had was our spiritual protection against a state and a society that hate us.

João: Can you talk about the ways in which this spiritual protection takes place? What happens in the moment when you know you're guided by this spiritual dimension? You mentioned the time your house was invaded by armed police officers.

Hamilton: Your intelligence is heightened and expanded. At that moment when they came for me in my house, I immediately understood what was happening. A week earlier we had been at the Nordeste de Amaralina neighborhood, where a pregnant woman had been forced into pornographic positions by cops. We denounced everything, and had the press cover it.

When the cops came, I was alone at home with my son, who at the time was a toddler. I looked out of the window and saw one of them had a machine gun—it looked homemade, probably something they seized from a drug dealer. In that moment, I called everyone I knew, and they showed up shortly thereafter. This can only be protection from another realm. I was ready to jump over into the surrounding houses with my son on my back, like a backpack—I had already spoken with him about it, as if it was a game. But many people arrived by car, by motorcycle, and the cops left. I don't know if I can explain it, but in practice, you become superhuman. I imagine a runaway enslaved person, without a map, without a weapon. Our spiritual strength shows up in those moments.

Andreia, for example, was nicknamed pejoratively Black superwoman (*super negona*) after an incident during a show in Barra. The police brutalized a young person and when I protested, they arrested me. Undeterred, Andreia confronted the police officers and hit a police officer's baton with her sandal. She then hit the cops, including a woman officer, whom she slapped and scratched. That called the attention of a lot of people. Now, if there was no reaction, if Andreia didn't confront them, who knows where they would have taken me, and what they would have done. Andreia did not accept the silence, and she reacted, she became the Black superwoman.

João: So this spiritual protection is the consciousness that, in the crucial moment, you are being protected.

Hamilton: Your ancestors accompany you; for that to happen, you have to be attuned to them. And in Rise Up we have this connection with the dead, we remember the impoverished Black people, we remember their cries. These people stay with us, they support us. I've had brothers from my Candomblé house tell me to stop talking about the dead, "They'll bring bad things for you."

I tell them they don't bring bad things to me—I'm taking care of their families, I'm keeping their memories alive.

I have a dream project of writing a book with the faces and the histories of each one of the people we accompanied, including the number of their burial site, so that they stay alive for the centuries ahead of us, and then they can return to earth and fulfill their life proposals.[6] It's very difficult for Black people to fulfill our proposals. And for me, it's all about fulfilling our proposals.

João: When we take into account the pervasiveness of violent death of Black people you both talk about, we have to emphatically reject the myth that Brazil, differently than the US, doesn't have a history and present marked by lynching. Lynching of Black people is pervasive in Brazil. I'm hearing your dream project as a description of a book based on your archives of lynchings.

Hamilton: I remember the death of Pit, who was one of the local criminal faction's founders. The police were after him, and then they killed him following a chase. We sent a document to the federal Human Rights office showing he was lynched. Pit was one of eight similar deaths, but his was more cruel because, following the chase and gunfire exchange, he turns himself in. His body shows up with the arms broken and a shot in the back of the head. But the police claim he was killed during the gunfire exchange. How can you say he was killed while he was shooting when his arms are broken and he's shot in the back of the head? There was no investigation.

Pressured by our protests and our work behind the scenes, the local police became somewhat more accountable around 2007–08. But then a Federal Police chief wrote in a major newspaper that the Bahia police are soft. The next day, Evangivaldo was killed with nine shots. We know he was no saint; he was a drug dealer, he was cruel, he beat up people. Still, we insist the state cannot be vengeful, it needs to follow the rule of law. That's why we don't have a democracy. While they dragged the bodies, the police sang their anthem in front of the mothers. The mothers of state victims are with us and like us because they see how committed we are.

We invented the general theory of failure because we weren't successful at anything. We didn't succeed in suing any of the police officers, we didn't change the police violent approach; rather the opposite, the police received more weapons, and people became more intimidated. We failed at everything. Maybe Andreia disagrees. I think we failed in our proposal of bringing freedom to our people. We're not going to be successful as long as we're asking for certain public policies and as long as we're expecting conscientious and caring institutions.

We're only going to be successful when the people who are harmed organize themselves. But organizations that are historically Black, or have a lot of Black people in them, don't want to get involved: soccer, church, Candomblé, and even the drug traffickers, who are the greatest providers of resources in our communities (cooking gas, schools, daycare centers, telephone, internet, etc.). We have to deal with all of that, it's not just the state in its raw force. We have to deal with our own people's cynicism. We are different because we're not giving up.

One of the mothers who, a few years ago, witnessed her son dragged and killed by the police, she called us about two weeks ago. She wanted to speak with Andreia. She didn't call asking us to organize a meeting in the neighborhood; she didn't call because we were able to get some compensation from the state for her son's death; she called because she likes us. It's difficult because people expect that we do everything. We tell them they need to get involved, you need to be in charge. Then there's another death, and three hundred people show up here, and there's an expectation that we'll do all the organization and mobilization.

João: In the inaugural ceremony yesterday, when Lula took office, there was a symbolically strong scene in which Black women, Black children, and people with disabilities were represented.[7] From the perspective of Rise Up or Die! how did you make sense of that moment?

Hamilton: Yesterday, after watching the entire event, I wrote an essay in which I say "hopelessness is a zeal." I wrote this because there's so much hope, happiness, euphoria for things that, for us, are merely symbolic. I'm saying this because we've been here before. It's the third time we're in this symbolism. We don't live in the symbolic world, we live in the real concrete world.

I'll give you an example. I don't drink alcohol, I stay sober. I don't use anything that alters the reality. In such a harsh world, it's hard to live like this. I think the energy during Lula's inauguration was beautiful, it was good. But we know there's the day after. When the carnival is over, we're left with reality. Many Rise Up people don't believe in any of this symbology. But Black people in general, we're too naive. Yet those who supposedly represent us in such spaces of power, they're not naive. They have a very well-defined project of power; they put their family members in those institutions, which will guarantee that they have much better prospects than most Black people: they will be able to get formal education, they'll have employment, they'll be financially stable.

But our concern is with the majority of our people, who is left with nothing. For us, as Andreia said, public policy is like a placebo. It has a psychological effect on us. You may have more buying power, you buy nice clothes, a TV, a refrigerator, but you don't buy land, you don't buy a house, you don't have financial investments, you don't leave a financial inheritance. I voted for Lula in 1989. This current moment is beautiful theater. But it doesn't reflect reality.

Andreia mentioned Snoop Doggy Dog compared Pelé to Muhammad Ali. But it's a bad comparison. Ali had a commitment toward his people. I've heard comparisons between Lula and Nelson Mandela. Lula is a white man. We Black people need to stop adoring white people. You look at his ministries, he put

Black people in symbolic posts devoid of power. What will a Human Rights minister do? For that position, Lula appointed a Black man, Silvio Almeida. What is Almeida going to do when I come to his office and say that I want to denounce Rui Costa, who is the current federal minister of Institutional Relations and was the governor of the state of Bahia, for genocide against Black people? Almeida may even find time to see me, and he may try to do something, but we know nothing will happen.

Then there's the Ministry of the Promotion of Racial Equality. The very notion of equality is harmful. The debate is rooted in an old discussion about whether Black people are human, and between two white men lawyers in particular, Rui Barbosa and Clovis Bevilaqua in the early 1900s.[8] And we are still debating equality. There's an elder MNU activist who used to say, "Black people want equality with whites, but whites don't want to be equal to Black people." Even the Landless Workers' Movement sent out a press release saying that social movements now need to be the government's base and strengthen it. For me, this makes no sense. That's why I feel isolated. In this conjuncture, there's no more space for us. We're going to have to forge our own space. We have to elaborate a new strategy for our struggle. We can't struggle like we did in 2005. We lived the pandemic apocalypse. We need to start over. We need a new birth.

We have a political obligation to mobilize people and communities, we need to develop oppositional thinking, and create spaces of joy, happiness, and abundance. Only then we'll be able to confront state and society. And when we do so, we'll have to confront the Black people who are the watchdogs. They don't appear in photos, but they're doing a lot of work behind the scenes. Some of them are truly excellent people; I respect them.

White people dominate those spaces of power. Lula's tactic was to throw himself toward the center right. That's why he got Alckmin as his vice president. The government's goal is to strengthen the market economy and guarantee minimum survival conditions for the people. But we don't expect land reform, we don't expect decarceration, we don't expect a deep debate about those topics, especially about public security.

João: Given the strong symbology and appeal of the Workers' Party, how do you approach the younger people? How do you talk about the weaknesses of the government program regarding Black people?

Hamilton: Some people think Rise Up doesn't have concrete proposals and that we only complain and lament. This also happens regarding our writing. I write literary fiction, and I talk about genocide, hunger, and hopelessness. When I'm among writers, at an event for example, I often hear a critique against my writing, "We need to talk about middle-class Black people." It's the same critique regarding our analysis. They say we only talk about terror, failure, and we don't present anything new. It reminds me of Malcolm X and how he was ostracized from the mainstream civil rights movement that dialogued with a white agenda. But Malcolm emphasized the need to have our own agenda, to have our own thought.

We try to show that our analysis and our literature come from the most wretched places, like prisons and impoverished and violent areas. But most people want to enjoy life, have a beer. It's like they're anesthetized. There's no political discussion—politics has been destroyed, it has become synonymous with elections and the monetary and power transactions that happen before, during, and after them.

We keep trying. We started a communitarian garden. We tell folks that they need to reject the food that's sold in the local supermarket, which is owned by whites who don't live here and who are just draining our resources away from our area. The food from that supermarket is making people sick: we get diabetes, high blood pressure. We live in a food desert. The food that's available is unhealthy and is not inspected by the consumer protection service. When we bring this up, no one is interested in talking about it. There's no alternative perspective. For a long time, we were a source of alternative thought here in Salvador, and that's because we talked about death, which is the most sensitive topic. We were in the cemeteries, we were in the Coroner's Office, we were in front of the police station. In all these places, we flirted with death. We were dealing with profound pain in the families of victims of police brutality. We hated the police and said so. We created a narrative for those experiences, a Black radical perspective, that had nothing to do with the narrative of human rights, which whites dominate.

We told whites that we accept their solidarity, but we also told them that they'd have no voice in our marches, rallies, and events. We organized a lot of local, state, and national events, as we mentioned earlier. In all of them, we collectively came up with alternatives models of safety, health, Black politics, society, and the state. White folks were not prepared for this. Frankly, Black people weren't either.

All this was very tiring and hurtful. I can't do it anymore: I can't deal with that pain, that tiredness, with having to crash into official meetings, go to military police stations. I can't deal with being persecuted and vilified by white and Black people. I don't have the energy anymore.

Now we're focusing on transforming our school into a great political school, a place where political thought will be debated and reverberated. It will also strengthen political practice in communities. Rise Up is turning eighteen this year, and along this time we forged our political perspective: we've been debating racism, death and genocide, the international character of the struggle, Quilombismo. Today we're convinced the perspective on antiblackness is fundamental. With revolutionary patience, we'll bring in and develop ties with people from all over Brazil as well as folks from South Africa, Europe, the US, and various parts of the Black Americas.

More immediately, we want to bring together people who think differently from us. Like bringing together the Crips and

Bloods. We want to sit around a table and reflect together. It wouldn't be the left or the right, it'd be us. It would be like an advanced nucleus of the struggle. We want to call for a great National Action Program, a political project for the country. There is no possibility for changing this country except via political action—it won't be via political parties or digital influence. Many social movements said they don't have a project for the country other than electing Lula. That is not our project.

João: You're thinking of a broad political front.

Hamilton: Exactly. There are folks in the south of Bahia already working the land; there's the hip-hop people. Our obstacle is the distrust of us, but we can get over it.

João: Andreia, what is Rise Up's analysis of this moment as Lula is inaugurated? It seems that we're going through a rapid revision of our recent history, in which people like Pelé, who recently passed in December 2022, are now people who, according to press commentators, had or inspired a critical analysis of Brazil's race relations despite being timid at best thoughout their lives around such issues.[9]

Andreia: It's important to point out that Black people like Pelé, Anielle Franco, and Sílvio Almeida are not a problem for us. They provide a shield for our greatest problem, which is white supremacy. We obviously don't want to disregard the experience of a Black woman like Franco. Rather, we want to emphasize that, in order to confront racism—to which the Lula administration claims it is committed—the process should have been different. Whose voice is being heard, and who's occupying high-level posts in the Ministry of Women, Family and Human Rights and the Ministry of Racial Equality? It feels like we've been through this before. Despite the Ministry of Racial Equality's recognition that there's an extermination of young Black people in course, genocide continues. I don't think filling posts with Black people will make any difference. But we may be surprised. Maybe people in those offices may facilitate, or may be sensitive to, various denunciations of police brutality and killings, the continued disappearance of young Black people, and how Black communities are impacted by these and other processes that lead to preventable death of Black people. Particularly the denunciations that originate in international organizations.

In relation to Pelé's death, as in the passing of other Black icons, his racial belonging was rendered invisible during his lifetime, or at least diluted. It happens to all of us. Pelé was treated like a king, which required that his African heritage and background be silenced, including the struggles that his father and mother, who were quite humble, went through in the interior of the Minas Gerais state, where the legacies of agricultural slavery and corrupt and violent politics certainly affected them.

As a dark-skinned person like him, my problem is not with Pelé, it's with white supremacy. It's always quite easy to blame a Black person for what they didn't do. He could have been more outspoken about racial issues, but then perhaps he wouldn't be treated and benefited like a king. Same thing with Anielle Franco, I don't want to criticize her. But we know there were other names of Black people with a longer political trajectory—including some who are part of the Workers' Party base—who are qualified and would try to radicalize the ministry. The work of white supremacy is extensive.

The same deradicalization happened in the state of Bahia. In preparation for the 2020 mayoral election, the Workers' Party discussed potential candidates. Due to the historical moment, Salvador being the largest Black city outside the African continent, proportionally, there was a sense that a Black woman should be the candidate. But instead of supporting Black women who had a trajectory in social movements, big political bosses, white men like Rui Costa and the senator Jaques Wagner, supported Denice Santiago Santos do Rosario, a Black Military Police Major who is also a psychologist. It seems to me that Anielle Franco and Silvio Almeida's presence is similar insofar as it is part of a white supremacist project that allows certain Black people to have some form of power.

João: Hamilton mentioned that he's exhausted and that he can't continue doing the same types of interventions he's been doing for decades. Do you feel the same way?

Andreia: From a woman's perspective, it's different. My mother, aunts, and sisters taught me to see the world in a particular manner. My relationship with Rise Up is the same as my relationship with my Black teenage son. At the end of each day, I'm exhausted. I look at what I had to endure, and I look at what needs to be done tomorrow.

I feel the same way as Hamilton about Rise Up in terms of the tiredness. But our exhaustion gives us perspective. It's a moment when we realize we can't go on like we did until now. It's necessary to bring in new people and build collectively, forging new paths.

I remember my mother when she looked at the empty pantry, two weeks into the month, and wondered how we'd make the next two weeks. It would have to be just rice and beans until the next month when my father's salary came in. I learned from her. Collectively, we evoke this kind of knowledge, and we figure it out. I remember my mother's tired gaze; but she persisted. It's part of me now, and we'll find a way.

Rise Up turned eighteen in 2023, and we're happy—not because we have a lot, but because we feel like we've done enough to explore new paths and harvest what we planted along the way. We're happy because, while striving for autonomy, we've been able to reorient ourselves. We can't go on like we did in the last eighteen years, which were of utmost importance. We spent many sleepless nights—I did many night shifts at work—

not knowing how we'd pay for the school's rent, how we'd offer children a snack, and so many other daily demands that were put on us with the expectation that we'd resolve things immediately.

Now we're looking at this differently, recognizing we need to strengthen ourselves. Today we can't carry as many rocks as we did, but those rocks have been placed. The corner stone is in place, and we need to continue building.

We've done so much that we never had time to celebrate some of our achievements; we didn't realize how many seeds we planted. With very limited resources, we put in a great investment of our time, and we had support from many people.

We can't really say we are tired; we have a continued commitment with so many people. Our lives continue to be devalued. The former Bahia governor, now a Lula administration minister, continues to belittle the twelve young people who were killed in Cabula. The victims' mothers are discouraged. Our role is to continue the struggle, not with false hope, but with a commitment to collectively build our future. With each name we're going to remember on February 6, 2023, on the eighth anniversary of the Cabula massacre, we're also evoking hope of a better collective future. Otherwise, the struggle is meaningless.

João: Can you talk about your vision of the future?

Andreia: I think we need to rescue the power that Black women have and built collectively. When we look at the mothers who lost their children to police brutality, despite all the sadness, they try to carry on with their daily lives. They help neighbors, they're active, they search for a light in their lives. It's very inspiring in the sense that we have to project a future and rescue this energy that we call the Comando Vital, which is the force that allows us to continue on, and continue building.

In their families, while women keep things moving, everyone's alright. They do the shopping, they do the planning, the cleaning, they come to meetings—they bake a cake and make coffee to bring to the meeting, they recognize everyone's in the struggle and that we need to eat. Today, I can see more clearly how the collective reconstruction takes place and the central place women have in it. In our school, we have a Formation Center, and it's a happy place, bright and beautiful. On the walls we have representations of our own history. We can't forget it; we can't think that we're restarting from scratch. We have the conditions from which to consolidate all the communitarian work that we've accomplished, and I think this is our vision of the future.

Yesterday, Sunday, we ran into Wagner, who was one of the fist students at the Winnie Mandela school. Today he's seventeen or eighteen years old. It struck us how vulnerable Wagner is, unfortunately. All we wanted was to protect him from so many forms of harm and danger. When we met him and his family, and we saw his smile, it brought home that the work is not done, but rather, that we have to press on. There's no end to the work. We have to consolidate this space as ours, where dark-skinned Black people are protected and are building collectively. We're building a legacy not only for the future, but also for the present everyday life. We're going to plant this seed in other communities. We're dealing with a continuous, gigantic, and complex problem, and we have to confront it—there's no other way. This is what is going to nourish us.

João: The concept of the Comando Vital indicates both the accumulation of political knowledge and how Black women have consistently found ways to guarantee community survival and therefore future generations. Your encounter with Wagner suggests an encounter with the future and what needs to be done. It helped me grasp the importance of the Comando Vital, and how it is rooted in ancestral knowledge women carry with them. It's quite a contrast to the perspective of men. Am I hearing some optimism here?

Andreia: I'm going to search for "optimism" in the dictionary because sometimes I think there are certain words that lose their meaning. I think what we have is pragmatism with relation to what's in front of us, not so much optimism. I was born in the midst of all this. I'm the heir of people who decided they'd insist in organizing themselves so that I could be where I am today, with a level of sanity and being able to make choices. I could make choices. I've been making choices in my fifty years of life, thanks to the choices my parents made, and their parents before, and so on.

The pragmatism that I mentioned is the same that I heard in the conversations between the women in my family. In family gatherings, when we were by ourselves as women, we discussed all kinds of matters and planned ahead. Often we had to come up with solutions to different types of problems, there was no other way. I carry that pragmatism, and I think that, as I mature, I'm learning to value it even more. We continue to dream—and this is also fundamental—but when we wake up from a dream and we have its memory, we have to be pragmatic as to how we implement the dream.

João: I'm hearing you describe a type of insistent pragmatism, one that doesn't give up even when faced with overwhelming circumstances.

Andreia: When mothers bring their newborns to protest in front of the Military Police or the Ministry of Public Security, that's the pragmatism I'm talking about. It's what needs to be done. I worked through many nights to generate much needed resources for Rise Up and then slept for three hours and went to an organizing activity in the prison. In the way that I understand my role in the collective, that's what needed to be done. When we risk ourselves in the confrontations with the police, it's the result of the collective struggle pragmatism that recognizes the necessity of opposition, resistance, and survival. It also insists in carrying forward our own project. This makes us believe in the possibility of doing something, a belief nourished in the practice. I don't think we can implement our vision in any space; what we proposed ourselves to do is only possible in certain spaces, and in those spaces we can protect and defend what we've done.

João: It seems that the Comando Vital, based on Black women's knowledge, is also a collective survival engineering: they know what needs to be done, and if they don't they'll invent something.

Andreia: Exactly. Those who stayed in Rise Up know we must restructure ourselves, and we'll find a way. There are so many anonymous Black women who guaranteed the survival of their family without any kind of support. They constructed some of their knowledge in the practice, and we also inherited knowledge from our elders.

My mother certainly didn't have a manual on how to raise four Black kids, and she had no instructions on how to make it possible that all four had choices and flourished. She learned in the process, relying on family, neighbors, friends. And simple things that she passed on to us: "If you eat everything at lunch, there's not going to be dinner." Simple things. "Put more water in the beans; divide up the food." These are things that my mother still says. The process is quite beautiful.

João: There's no ready manual, but maybe it's available at some level. I imagine your manual is similar to your mother's, which was similar to the one her parents had. And then it gets expanded and adapted?

Andreia: Certainly, this vital force is passed on from generation to generation. Various codes and instructions are transmitted that way, which we grasp only with time. Some of the things my mother said, I get it now: when I think about groceries for the month, my son's school supplies, and when we had to come up with snacks for twenty-seven kids at the school.

At the Winnie Mandela school, how were we going to build a routine, a curriculum? We had no help from education specialists. Based on the children we knew, including my own, we came up with a routine: when students arrived, they started with the homework. Then there's a collective moment and a time to read in group. Then we taught them how to wash their hands, brush their teeth—there was a session on personal hygiene.

As we got cohorts with older kids, we also talked about sexual development, including body changes in puberty—at that point we got help from women who had expertise on those topics. As we developed our school, some of the many codes that were passed to us began to make sense and were applied; we drew from the manual, as it were. We carry many of the codes and the manual with us, I agree with you.

We talked about the letters my father wrote. That's how I look into the future—as he looked, as my mother looked: projecting, constructing. When we look at the manifestos we wrote for each of the annual marches, we talk about what we accomplished, but we also talk about what we want to do. So they're letters for the future, they're manifestos of our continuity.[10]

João: Every time I've been at the school, I felt like I was in a spaceship, and now I see why. It has to do with this vision of the future, in this insistent engineering that refuses to stop.

Andreia: It's good to hear that. There's the nagging thought that maybe we're not doing enough, or not doing it right. We revisit history, we reflect on it, and we retell our own history—that nourishes us. That's why it's important to write about what we have accomplished, it brings renewed energy. We've done so much that often we forget about it, it gets lost.

João: Hamilton, what is your dream? What does it look like?

Hamilton: I have a dream in three dimensions: short term, medium term, long term. The latter two dimensions are in my latest book. In the short term, it's the remodeling of the Rise Up headquarters to make it a dignified space, a beautiful and inviting space where we debate and exchange knowledge, we experiment artistically and scientifically. We'll spread the ideas from the Winnie Mandela school.

In 2004 and 2005, during our Provocation Wednesdays we were already thinking about this Pan-Africanist school. At this point, I don't think it's as much Africanist as it is quilombista, from a radical experience of Africans in Brazil, which we continue to develop.

Medium term, we have to expand our experience of struggle to new territories, we're calling it the Os Novos Quilombos de Zumbi (New Zumbi Quilombos, from a Caetano Veloso song). This project involves the fields of health, law, literature, arts, and agriculture. We're going to bring books, ideas, debates to the communities that today are completely emptied of dignity.

At eighteen, Rise Up or Die! has reached its adulthood. We've reached a point at which when there's a police homicide of a Black person, there's widespread lamentation. The press, the academics, folks in the streets, they talk about it, but there's no movement. It's as if an outer space alien landed, killed the person, and left: there's no cause, there's no one responsible for the death.

We're desperate and hopeless. We want to go to those places that are the most challenged and say that there are possibilities for us to build communities in which we can breathe, we can think independently, and we can dream. To dream is an indispensable tool. The African deities, all of them, they dream. When we dream, we also realize the dream. As things stand, I don't see any possibility for Black people in one hundred years. As Fred Aganju says, worse days will come, and they're already here. In Salvador, Porto Alegre, São Paulo, there's already water shortages, and reservoirs are at their limit.

João: I'm hearing that the quilombo you dream of is mostly, if not entirely, composed of dark-skinned Black people, who would be the initiative's political and theoretical agents. Is that correct?

Hamilton: In my book of fiction, *Bantu Machine,* dark-skinned Black people can be killed at any time, and there are no consequences because they don't have any value in the Enclosed City. They're only valued in the quilombo, that's why they're constantly fleeing the city.

Nonblack people don't have a say in this project. If they're allies, and they have resources, they should contribute.

The lighter-skinned people have associations with spheres of power and live a more tranquil life; they try to promote dialogue between whites and Black people, and they tell Black people that, if you don't revolt, the system is good and won't kill you. So the book is for Black people. If you're able to build a quilombo from a quilombista perspective, the strategies will be quilombista, and the affect and love will be quilombista too.

Light-skinned Black people need to define themselves. They need to say what they want and what side they're on. Sometimes I look at light-skinned people's social media, and they're not in places where there's a Black majority, they don't want that. I think no one wants to be with us. Maybe because we're too loud, too angry.

I was brought up in the Black movement of the 1970s. In its bylaws, there was something that caught my attention, and today I wonder about it. It said, "Black is the person who has traits that are typical of the race." It was a very broad definition, but I think it included mixed-race Black people like my great grandmother, who was considered *sarará* (mixed). I don't think the definition included people like Antonio Carlos Magalhães Neto, a politician who claims to be mixed.[11]

Aílton Krenak, an Indigenous intellectual, said that in the 1990s, in face of genocide, it was decided that the vital strategy of survival for Indigenous people was to marry and have as many children as possible. It's the same for us, to continue existing and dreaming, we need to have Black children.

According to the Brazilian Census, dark Black people like me are only seven percent of the population. We're not the majority, like the Black movement claims. We are unmistakably Black. Ask Andreia if she has any doubt. But there are light-skinned people who say, "I discovered myself Black in college" or "I discovered myself Black when I came to Salvador." Dark-skinned people are stopped in the streets, the police look at us differently. To this day, when I'm surrounded by white people, I feel out of place.

In 2020, there were many live virtual events on Black literature. But there were no Black people. Both Jovina Souza, a literary scholar, and Andreia called my attention to this. We feel it on our skin. Light-skin privilege is everywhere, including in the prisons, where the leadership also tends to be lighter-skinned.

I'm not saying that a light-skinned Black person doesn't suffer. Yet racism's sequelae impact dark-skinned people more directly. You look at who's incarcerated, and you'll see they are mostly dark-skinned. On the other hand, in academia, most Black people are light-skinned. And when I'm near them, they clutch their belongings. It's very draining. I catch myself policing myself, and I'm concerned about everyone around me. I don't know if there are people who can live at peace with that, but I can't.

Recently, I went to a clinic for a consultation, and the doctor kept the door open the entire time. She only opened the door when I was there. It's very hard for us. Doctors don't touch us. And some of them say they're Black—at least at the university, where they claim racial quotas by invoking a parent or grandparent who is Black. I feel that light-skinned folks are not willing to engage in any kind of radical struggle, and that's because they have a lot to lose. Curuzu, the neighborhood where I grew up, is the place where there's more Black people in Salvador. There, the lighter-skinned people have the larger houses; the police don't bother them.

João: Andreia, you mentioned that you dream, and that when you wake up and remember the dream, pragmatically you have to figure out how to implement it. What do you dream of?

Andreia: We dream a lot. The school was a dream. The idea of having our own building was a dream, but there were other demands that were put on the backburner. In order to accomplish all those things, we have to dream first, and without the dream there would be no pragmatic strategy. Even after we started the school, we didn't know from where the rent for the second month was going to come. We bought a bunch of things on credit, and our credit card was done. We dream about having a communitarian organization buzzing with Black people.

I imagine that inside the Palmares quilombo everything was not wonderful all the time; the same during the uprisings. Things are complex, and so is our presence in the world. The people who came before me, my blood ancestors, they must have suffered immeasurably for me to get here. We're also going to go through many trials. That's why it's so critical to dream. We dream with our feet on the ground—we must continue to build, but we have to be realistic, and even expect internal betrayals. We have to anticipate having the rug pulled from under our feet by those who were supporting us.

We continue to seek articulations with folks who study, who are scholars, but they seem to distance themselves from the reality of the carceral system, the reality of Black women, of impoverished people, who are often in the same areas where we live. In our own neighborhood we have several unhoused people, people going through food insecurity. Since the turn of the year, the area has been under siege. There's a dispute between the police and drug dealers. When I visit certain areas around here, to offer medical consultation—areas you can't drive to—I give a three-day notice so that everyone knows it's me that's coming, and I'm not mistaken for someone else.

What we dream of, what we visualize, is to continue going to those places we've been going to in the last eighteen years and to continue building. Those places still don't have basic sanitation, they flood when it rains. People go hungry. In truth, this is what nourishes us.

My main dream, which is becoming more crystalized as we talk, is to have a group of Black women who are empowered and able to produce our own history, starting with their families, their communities. It would be a multitude of Black women, organized and conscious. It would be an army of Black women. The image that comes to mind is that of a woman with a child in one arm and a rifle in the other. But at other times, it will be food instead of the rifle; a book; a blanket. When we organize our events, we see this potential that is stored in Black women's strength that sustain their families and communities.

That's the image I have for our quilombo. People producing their own food, in a clean place, unpolluted, worshiping Orixás and ancestrality—this soothes my heart, and excites me. But it requires that we go plant our feet in the mud, jump over open sewage, to provide food for those in need. All the while maintaining the communitarian project in which we discuss possible futures.

We need to resignify the model of the state which we have internalized, which only benefits white people. We need to cut ourselves from those concepts of governmentality. There are more than seventy million people who go through moderate food insecurity.[12]

This is a long-term project, and it involves bringing more people on board. We meet people in the street who say, "I want to visit the school. I was in jail. When I was away from you, I could see what you were doing and what you were saying. I now understand, and I know how I can help. I have one day in the week."

So we're building. The problem is complex, and its roots are profound. Unlike white people, we can't put a number to our small victories. We're going to bring more people out of the mud. It's a possible reality, and Black women provide examples. They're looking ahead with their children. We know of a family with five women, no adult men. Some of their companions died, others were incarcerated or became drug addicts. The women stayed with the kids. They do domestic work, they hustle, and in between their daily activities they take the kids to school; they organize second-hand clothes sales in their home, and we help them with basic foods. It's women like them that make up the army I dream of.

"POETRY OF INSURRECTION, AESTHETICS OF BLACK AUTONOMY"

Dylan Rodríguez

Rise Up or Die! is not merely a social movement, community formation, or explosively experimental expression of Black autonomy. It is also far more than a radical rejoinder to the stale strategic, theoretical, and ideological frameworks structuring human rights campaigns, civil reforms, and inclusivist mobilizations for access to state power and adjoining public and corporate infrastructures. Within and beyond its singular capacity to stoke confrontation with the institutions, political assumptions, and liberal compromises (and compradors) that capture and discipline Black freedom to conform to existing societal regimes, Rise Up or Die! is an ungovernable, activated imaginary. It is a proliferating poetics of Black liberationist autonomy that apprehends—as it enacts—the insurrectionary imperative that stalks a hemispheric Civilization project.

Insurrection, in this case self-determined and rigorously theorized Black liberationist counter-war, is primary to Andreia, Hamilton, and Rise up or Die!'s way of (non-)being as alter-being—a collective creativity that resists static definition while constantly generating refusals, self-determinations, collective nourishment, and the activating contagions of Black radical fearlessness. Make no mistake: this is alter-being formed in antiblack terror, saturated by everyday mourning over the casualties extracted by Brazil's—and the planet's—normalized commitment to eviscerating Black bodies, Black places, and Black life. Here, fearlessness is the symptomatic expression of deeply shared courage and the unshakeable militancy of Black love as transgenerational, transhistorical, time-bending insurgent power.

Simultaneously, if there is an initial lesson to be taken from the previous pages, it is that insurrection is a permanent condition of necessity for (dark-skinned) Black people and thus exceeds the civilities of *the political* and the incrementalism of *negotiation.* When Andreia echoes Frantz Fanon's venerable conceptualization of colonial-chattel antiblackness as the epidermalization of foundational Civilizational violence—her lyric is, "You carry Africa on your skin" (p. 51)—she is reciting a refrain of irreconcilability: the insurrection imperative is a time-bending, perpetual obligation to destroy the flimsy, insulting, and often maiming or deadly apparatuses of condescending solicitation, piecemeal empowerment, and earnest civil coalition that attempt to domesticate Black alter-being and obliterate the Black quilombo in favor of absorption into a wretched nation-state. For Hamilton, this means that when the well-meaning, respectable agents of political (or cultural, or academic . . .) inclusivity and empowerment "come to Rise Up wanting to change us, wanting to make us more polished and recognizable," the only feasible response is to remind them, "That never works." Then what? "We tell them to leave." (p. 110)

As I read this book, I was participating in a small study group with people from around the US who were reading (and re-reading) George Jackson's *Blood in My Eye* (1972). (Notably, no one in the group other than me was employed as a university faculty member or "academic.") There is something about this ongoing historical moment that convenes new, old, and embryonic communities around the insurrectionist poetics inscribed by the living Black archive of guerrilla organizers, teachers, artists, and intellectuals who actively dream—and concretely strategize—the end of Civilization. It may be appropriate, then, to consider Jackson's fleeting reflection on the embodied, shared preconditions of Black revolutionary activity as a posthumous, diasporic endorsement of Rise Up or Die!'s changing relationship and response to collective trauma, normalized genocidal antiblackness, and the irreducible praxis of Black mourning: "We've organized our thoughts and trained our bodies for the ordeal of 'gravedigging . . .' If people are to understand and relate to revolutionary violence, they must first be educated into an acceptance of the fact that there is no alternative, or that the alternative is less inviting than a fight."[1]

While simplistic, one-dimensional interpretations of Jackson's carceral—and public—pedagogy might reduce such passages to prescriptions borne of bloodlust and suicidal adventurism, the unfolding of Rise Up or Die!'s praxis demonstrates how Black self-determination, Black collective (and individual) self-defense, transgenerational Black wisdom, and autonomous Black strategic infrastructure *are already encountered by Civilization and its* self-appointed *representatives as "violence."* And if nonblack (and some Black) audiences to such streams of Black radical and revolutionary activity were to be fully honest with themselves, they would perhaps admit that such reactions contain an unsettling kernel of truth even as they wallow in the mire of political repression, liberal dismissal, and (dishonest, hypocritical) moral condemnation: Black alter-being *does* signify the obsolescence and collapse, if not the destruction and Black liberated aftermath of the nation-state, including and especially the compulsory dreams (nightmares) of multiculturalist "democracy," inclusive governance, and reformed, twenty-first-century approaches to Civilizational progress.

Hamilton thus narrates the perpetual insurrection imperative as an expression of collective love, courage, respect, and honor *within the Jacksonian "fight."* This activation of imagination shatters the prestige of the colonial, antiblack order and its everyday institutions, including the police, local government, civil and nongovernmental organizations, and various representatives of neoliberal corporate power: "We wanted to speak with Black people in their communities, and show them that, together, we can fight this gigantic monster. We succeeded." (p. 71) Further expanding the historical and archival scope of this fight, Andreia advances a communitarian tradition that recasts Civilization as alien, alienated territory that requires relentless Black study and analysis precisely because it cannot and will not withstand the insurrection of alter-being that confronts antiblack omni-death with a surging Black praxis that is everywhere and everything— materially, aesthetically, and otherwise:

> I chose a medical specialty that seeks a communitarian approach to health and disease, which is related to a communitarian approach to fighting racism . . . [I]t's impossible to fight racism alone. I conceptualize myself as part of a collective history. My own family confirms it and acts accordingly. We don't raise ourselves by ourselves; we don't raise our kids by ourselves; we can't overcome the daily difficulties by ourselves. Collectively we learn things, including how to take care of ourselves and others. My medical communitarian approach allows an understanding of the ways in which everything that's around us—society, the environment, institutions—impacts an individual's existence. It's an African prism both in terms of analysis and of care. (p. 56)

It is worth affirming, from my position as a longtime student and teacher, that this book is a precious gift that also exerts an urgent demand: you must find ways to create or participate in the endless, collective activities that wage counter-war against the occupying, war-making, genocidal beast surrounding you, if not within, then in caring relation and serious coordination with the Black liberationist insurrection imperative.

Rise Up or Die! is the poetry of the Black guerrilla fugitive/warrior/caretaker—a (trans-)gendered figure that is both intimately present and fundamentally de-individualizing: the insurrection itself is a poem, always undergoing revision, multimodal and multivocal, planned and improvised, inscribed by a growing, unnamed, interconnected commune of practitioners whom João identifies as a spreading Black quilombo. (p. 10) Rise Up or Die! may be partly or entirely illegible to nonblack positions and experiences (as well as to Black liberal and respectability-oriented blocs), but its irruptive aesthetic-material presence will nonetheless indelibly mark the space and define the moment.

ENDNOTES

PREFACE: "WHEN LIBERATION KNOCKS, OPEN THE DOOR TO RISE UP, DIE, REBIRTH"

1   For an analysis of the Captive Maternal, see Joy James, *New Bones Abolition: Captive Maternal Agency and the (After)Life of Erica Garner*, Common Notions, 2023.

INTRODUCTION

1   For context on the emergence, past and current outlook and practice of Rise Up, see the various creative essays and books by Andreia Santos: *Olhar Por Entre Grades, Vidas em Poemas* (Salvador: Reaja Editora, 2020); *Tempo em Mim* (Salvador: Reaja Editora, 2023); and by Hamilton Borges: *Teoria Geral do Fracasso* (Salvador: Quilombo X, 2017); *Salvador, Cidade Túmulo* (Salvador: Reaja Editora, 2018); *Salvador, Tomb City: Black Genocide and Anti-Black Racism in Brazil* (Salvador: Reaja Publishing Co., 2018); *O Livro Preto de Ariel* (Salvador: Reaja Editora, 2019); *Libido, Dendê, & Melanina* (Salvador: Reaja Editora, 2020); and *Bantu Machine: O Homen que Queria Ser Branco.* (Salvador: Reaja Editora, 2023). Rise Up's website contains several essays going back to 2012 that provide invaluable information on the organization's perspective as key events unfolded: https://reajanas-ruas.blogspot.com. Ethnographies in English on some of Salvador's Black geographies and political struggles include Keisha-Khan Perry, *Black Women Against the Land Grab: The Fight for Racial Justice in Brazil* (Minneapolis: University of Minnesota Press, 2013); Erica Williams, *Sex Tourism in Bahia: Ambiguous Entanglements* (Urbana: University of Illinois Press, 2013); and Christen Smith, *Afro-Paradise: Blackness, Violence, and Performance in Brazil* (Urbana: University of Illinois Press, 2016), which presents analyses of Rise Up.

2   Andreia Beatriz Silva Santos, Fábio Nascimento-Mandingo, Amy Chazkel, "React or Be Killed: The History of Policing and the Struggle Against Anti-Black Violence in Salvador, Brazil," *Radical History Review* 137 (2020): 157–175; Andreia Beatriz Silva Santos, "Horror Racial e a Brutalidade Policial: Quotidiano das Sequelas que Atingem Mulheres Negras," *Reaja ou Será Morto/Reaja ou Será Morta*, March 16, 2022, https://reajanasruas.blogspot.com.

3   The concept of sequela also provides a generative framework when put in dialogue with theoretical and political perspectives that build on the finding of the present-ness of slavery in contemporary formations of sociability, state, and empire. In the US, such perspectives emerge in essays and monographs by Angela Davis (institutional memory of slavery and the prison industrial complex), Orlando Patterson (slavery and social death), Joy James (neo-slavery), and Saidiya Hartman (the afterlife of slavery), among others.

4   Abdias do Nascimento, *Brazil, Mixture or Massacre?: Essays on the genocide of a Black People* (Dover, MA: Majority Press, 1989).

5   Historian and longtime activist Joel Rufino dos Santos (1941–2015) locates the origins of the Black movement in Brazil in 1931, with the foundation of the Frente Negra Brasileira (FNB) [Brazilian Black Front], which opposed the hegemonic racial democracy myth. While critical of the racial democracy ideology, and denouncing racism and social inequalities, FNB's objective, however, was to integrate Black people into Brazilian society; it was a national organization that was both assimilationist and nationalist. Its motto, not unlike that of fascist organizations in Europe and the Americas, was "God, Nation, Race, and Family." Between 1931 and 1937—when it was closed down by the dictatorship of Getúlio Vargas—its membership varied between forty and two hundred thousand people. See Joel Rufino dos Santos, "A Luta Organizada Contra o Racismo," in *Atrás do Muro da Noite; Dinâmica das Culturas Afro-Brasileiras*, Wilson do Nascimento Barbosa (Org.) (Brasília: Ministério da Cultura/ Fundação Cultural Palmares, 1994). See also Florestan Fernandes, *A Integração do Negro na Sociedade de Classes* (São Paulo: Editora Con-

tracorrente, [1964] 2021). The various newspapers and magazines of the Black press of the late 1800s and early 1900s were critical to the emergence of the FNB. See, for example, Ana Flávia Magalhães Pinto, *Imprensa Negra do Século XIX* (São Paulo: Selo Negro, 2010). There are several studies that analyze the emergence of MNU, a sample of which include: Lélia Gonzalez, "The Unified Black Movement: A New Stage in Black Political Mobilization," in *Race, Class, and Power in Brazil*, Pierre-Michel Fontaine (ed.) (Center for Afro-American Studies, University of California, Los Angeles 1985), 120–134; David Covin, *The Unified Black Movement in Brazil, 1978–2002* (Jefferson, NC: McFarland, 2006); Michael Hanchard, *Orpheus and Power: The Movimento Negro of Rio de Janeiro and São Paulo, Brazil, 1945–1988* (Princeton, NJ: Princeton University Press, 1994); also by Hanchard (ed.), *Racial Politics in Contemporary Brazil* (Durham: Duke University Press, 1999); Petrônio Domingues, "Movimento Negro Brasileiro: Alguns Apontamentos Históricos," *Tempo* 12, no. 23 (2007): 100–122; Amílcar Araújo Pereira, "O Mundo Negro: A Constituição do Movimento Negro Contemporâneo no Brasil (1970–1995)." PhD dissertation, Universidade Federal Fluminense, Rio de Janeiro, 2010; and *O Mundo Negro: Relações Raciais e a Constituição do Movimento Negro Contemporâneo no Brasil* (Rio de Janeiro: FAPERJ, 2013).

6 On the FNB, see endnote 5, above. For critiques of the racial democracy ideology, see, for example, Lélia Gonzalez, "Racismo e Sexismo na Cultura Brasileira," *Revista Ciências Sociais Hoje*, ANPOCS (1984): 223–244; Beatriz Nascimento, *Uma História Feita por Mãos Negras: Relações Raciais, Quilombos, e Movimentos.* Alex Rats (ed.) (Rio de Janeiro: Zahar. 2021); Abdias do Nascimento, *Brazil, Mixture or Massacre?* (Dover, MA: The Majority Press, 1989).

7   Rise Up's notion of Quilombismo draws from Abdias do Nascimento, "Quilombismo: An Afro-Brazilian Political Alternative," *Journal of Black Studies* 11, no. 2 (1980): 141–178; and Beatriz Nascimento, *Uma História Feita por Mãos Negras: Relações Raciais, Quilombos, e Movimentos.* Alex Rats (ed.) (Rio de Janeiro: Zahar, 2021)

8 Borges, *Bantu Machine.*

9   Bruno de Freitas Moura, "Maior Presença de Negros No País Reflete Reconhecimento Racial," *Agência Brasil*, December 24, 2023, https://agenciabrasil.ebc.com.br.

10   Marta Cavallini, "Proporção de Pretos e Pardos entre Pobres Chega ao Dobro em Relação aos Brancos, mostra o IBGE," *G1*, November 11, 2022, https://g1.globo.com.

11   Leonardo Vieceli, "64,2 milhões vivem em lares com insegurança alimentar no Brasil," *Folha de S.Paulo*, April 25, 2024, https://www1.folha.uol.com.br.

12   "Análise sobre a diferença entre brancos, pretos e pardos no Saeb," *IEDE*, November 21, 2020, https://www.portaliede.com.br.

13   Frantz Fanon states, "I should constantly remind myself that the real *leap* consists in introducing invention into existence." *Black Skin, White Masks.* Trans. Charles Markmann. (New York: Grove Press, [1952] 1967), 229.

14   Human is capitalized to mark its modern origins; see Moon-Kie Jung and João Costa Vargas, *Antiblackness* (Durham: Duke University Press, 2021).

15   This is an idea developed by Frank Wilderson in, for example, *Afropessimism* (New York: Liveright, 2020).

16   Fred Aganju Santiago, "Boletim de Luta Campanha Reaja ou Será Morta/o: A Marcha Fora de Controle," *Reaja ou Será Morto/Reaja ou Será Morta*, August 27, 2014, https://reajanasruas.blogspot.com. Since 2005, Rise Up articulates its own concept of genocide, drawing from and impacting the ongoing debate on the theme in Brazil; some of their essays on genocide, often in connection to their marches, Against the Genocide of Black People, appear on their website: https://reajanasruas.blogspot.com. On the debate and definitions of genocide as it applies to the collective experiences of Black people, see for example William Patterson, *We Charge Genocide: The Historic Petition to the United Nations for Relief for a Crime of the United States government against the Negro People* (New York: Civil Rights Congress, 1951); Nascimento, *Mixture or Massacre?;* João Costa Vargas, *Never*

Meant to Survive: Genocide and Utopias in Black Diaspora Communities (Langham, MD: Rowman & Littlefield, 2008), and "Genocídio" in *Dicionário das Relações Éthnico-Raciais Contemporâneas.* Eds. Flávia Rios, Marcio André dos Santos, Alex Ratts (Brasília: Editora Perspectiva), 335–350; Ana Flauzina, *Corpo Negro Caído no Chão: O Sistema Penal e o Projeto Genocida do Estado Brasileiro* (Rio de Janeiro: Contraponto, 2008).

17 Nascimento, *Mixture or Massacre?*

18 On Brazil's foundational hatred of Black people, see for example Jaime Amporo Alves and João Costa Vargas, "Polis Amefricana: para uma desconstrução da 'América Latina' e suas geografias sociais antinegras," *Latitude* 17, no. 1 (2023): 57–82.

19 Audre Lorde, "The Uses of Anger: Women Responding to Racism," in *Sister Outsider: Essays and Speeches* (Trumansburg, NY: Crossing Press, 1984), 115–125.

20 Both statements will reappear and gain context in this book's extended narratives.

21 Luiza Bairros, born in Porto Alegre in 1953, obtained her doctorate in Sociology at Michigan State University. A historic and central figure of the MNU, Bairros was the minister of Brazil's Secretariat for the Promotion of Racial Equality (2011–2014). She passed on July 12, 2016. See "Luiza Helena Bairros in Memoriam (1953–2016)," *Internationl Political Science Association,* July 13, 2016, https://www. ipsa.org.

22 For a similar critique in the US, see, for example, INCITE! (ed.), *The Revolution will not be Funded: Beyond the* Non-Profit *Industrial Complex* (Durham: Duke University Press, [2007] 2017).

23 See Pereira, "O Mundo Negro," 176–178. Interviews with Ferreira contain the "elite of the elite" quotation.

24 On Black study, see, for example, Stefano Harney and Fred Moten, *The Undercommons: Fugitive Planning & Black Study* (Brooklyn: Minor Compositions, 2013).

25 Pereira, "O Mundo Negro," 209.

26 This critique of liberal democracy is similar to reflections that connect democracy and the ongoing state warfare against Black people and marginalized groups in the US. See, for example, George Jackson, *Blood in My Eye* (Baltimore: Black Classic Press, 1990); Joy James (ed.), *Warfare in the American Homeland: Policing and Prison in a Penal Democracy* (Durham: Duke University Press, 2007); Dylan Rodríguez, *White Reconstruction: Domestic Warfare and the Logics of Genocide* (New York: Fordham University Press, 2021).

27 Borges, *Bantu Machine*, 99.

CHAPTER 1
BEGINNINGS

1 Candomblé is a religion Black Brazilians have elaborated since the sixteenth century. It draws from traditional African religions practiced by several African peoples including the Yoruba, Bantu, and Fon. Candomblé is organized in autonomous *terreiros* (houses), which aren't subodinated to a central authority. The religion venerates *orixás*, spirits that are subordinated to a transcendent creator god, Olodumaré. Individuals are believed to have a guiding orixá who informs their personality. Practitioners meet in houses whose main authority is a *mãe de santo* (priestess) or *pai de santo* (priest).

2 An Ekedi is a female initiate of the Candomblé religion. She takes care of the Orixá, a divine spirit sent by the supreme creator to assist humans within a *terreiro*. This feminine attribution is often the highest executive/administrative position.

3 A singer whose elaborate costumes and androgynous performances became a landmark of oppositional culture during the dictatorship.

4 Serviço Nacional de Aprendizagem Comercial, National Service of Commercial Learning, a public professionalization institution.

5   Ilê Aiyê, a Salvador carnival bloc founded in 1974 and based in the Curuzu/Liberdade neighborhood. Stressing Black pride, it allows only Black people to parade with the group.

6   "Olha ai, olha ai, olha ai a promoção da tropa de choque da Polícia Militar: chupe uma bala de escopeta e tenha um encontro marcado com o diabo!"

7   Nilma Lino Gomes, *O Movimento Negro Educador: Saberes Construídos Nas Lutas por Emancipação* (São Paulo: Editora Vozes, 2017).

8   Publicly funded restaurants offering healthy and affordable meals to city residents.

9   Primarily organized by the MNU, the 1995 March Against Racism, For Equality and Life congregated Black organizations and their allies in Brasília to protest racism and celebrate the 300th anniversary of Quilombo leader Zumbi dos Palmares. It is estimated that about forty thousand activists from all parts of Brazil came to the nation's capital on November 20, constituting the largest Black demonstration held in Brazil. See *Encyclopedia.com*, s.v. "Movimento Negro Unificado," https://www.encyclopedia.com.

10 Helena Greco (1916–2011), who graduated in Pharmacy at the Federal University of Minas Gerais in 1937, was founder and director of the Women's Movement for Amnesty (MFPA) in the state of Minas Gerais. In 1982, she was the first Workers' Party city councilperson elected in the state capital, Belo Horizonte, where she had two tenures, until 1992. See https://wikipeacewomen.org.

11 José Luiz Lisboa, "Trio preso durante falsa blitz em BH é integrante da Le Coq," *O Tempo*, April 3, 2016, https://www.otempo.com.br.

12 Founded in 1988, Geledés, the Black Women's Institute, is a political organization of Black women based in São Paulo. See https://www.geledes.org.br.

13 In Candomblé, mãe de santo is one's spiritual mother.

14 Rio Grande do Sul is the Brazilian state with the greatest proportion of white people.

15 On Rebouças (1839–1898), see Daniel Helton, "André Rebouças," *Black Past*, March 22, 2018, https://www.blackpast.org.

16 Patricia Marques, "Há 37 anos, Deise Nunes era eleita a primeira Miss Brasil negra da história," *Itatiaia*, May 17, 2023, https://www.itatiaia.com.br.

17 Jurandir Freire Costa, "Hermógenes e Reinaldo, mortos com 15 tiros,"*Folha de S. Paulo*, July 3, 1994, https://www1.folha.uol.com.br.

18 Bruna Caetano, "Uma história oral do Movimento Negro Unificado por três de seus militantes," *Brasil de Fato*, April 5, 2019, https://www.brasildefato.com.br.

19 *Brown University Library,* accessed on April 30, 2024, https://library.brown.edu. See also Alvaro Costa e Silva, "Pasquim e seu choque de egos revolucionaram a imprensa, mosta livro," *Folha de S. Paulo*, May 10, 2022, https://www1.folha.uol.com.br.

20 Mark Day, "Sr. Dorothy Stang, martyred American nun, remembered at Amazon synod," *National Catholic Reporter*, December 18, 2019, https://www.ncronline.org.

21 For an interview with Hamilton about the origins of Rise Up or Die! done by the newspaper Irohìn, see "Entrevista: Reja nasceu nas ruas," *Fundação Cultural Palmares*, June 19, 2007, https://www.palmares.gov.br.

22 For the controversy about flags, see Coordenação Nacional de Entidades Negras (CONEN), "Nota da Conen sobre a agressão de Reaja," *Portal Geledés*, September 1, 2015, https://www.geledes.org.br; for greater context, see Hamilton Borges, "A Marcha contra o Genocídio do Povo Negro Incomoda os inimigos," *Portal Geledés*, September 1, 2015, https://www.geledes.org.br.

23 "Bahia sediará Encontro Nacional da Juventude Negra," *Vermelho.* June 24, 2007, https://vermelho.org.br. In 2005, there had been

several national marches organized by Black collectives, including Zumbi + 10; See Vargas, *Denial of Antiblackness.*

24 On the death of Negro Blul, as well as of other persons Rise Up supported, see its website at https://reajanasruas.blogspot.com.

25 "The Lemos Brito Penitentiary was built in the 1950s, in Salvador's Mata Escura neighborhood. It was built to hold 771 people but presently it has 1550 prisoners, which are divided into four units. In the state of Bahia, it is the largest facility in which people fulfill their sentences in a closed regime (*regime fechado*)." Andreia Beatriz Silva dos Santos, "Identificação dos problemas de Saúde entre pessoas privadas de liberdade," *Revista de APS* 23, no. 1 (2020): 214.

26 See Giovanna Xavier, "Zeferina," *Enslaved.org*, May 31, 2017, https://enslaved.org.

27 See Rute Pina, "Cacique Babau, liderança indígena tupinambá, é preso em Ilhéus (BA)," *Brasil de Fato*, April 11, 2016, https://www.brasildefato.com.br.

28 See an analogous phenomenon in the US prison system in Vargas, *Denial of Antiblackness.*

29 Andreia worked as a medical doctor inside the Lemos Brito prison between 2007–2023; in 2005, she worked in the same prison as part of Rise Up's project Culture and Health Between Walls (Cultura e Saúde Intramuros).

30 "Presidente da Comissão Interamericana de Direitos Humanos Inicia Visita ao Brasil," *OEA*, June 30, 2005, https://www.oas.org.

31 See, by Fred Aganju, "Balanço Estratégico de Uma Teoria Geral do Fracasso," *Coletivo Das Lutas*, May 18, 2015, https://daslutas.wordpress.com.

32 The translation would be something like, "My brotherly people advance the universe, in the effective song that surpasses the barrier of the sun, and when echoed this song is like an ebolition created by the power of a sacred and very faithful Ashante people in the center

south of the Confederation commanded by Osei Tutu ile ayie who births in matter love for life."

33 "Quilombolas Communities in Brazil," *Comissão* Pró-Índio *de São Paulo*, March 2024, https://cpisp.org.br.

34 Jaques Wagner won the election and was the governor of Bahia between 2007–2015.

35 More on this event below.

36 Fátima Oliveira, *Saúde da População Negra: Brasil, Ano 2001* (Brasília: Organização Pan-Americana da Saúde, 2003).

37 On sexual terror, see for example, Ana Flauzina and Thula Pires, "Uma conversa de Pretas Sobre Violencia Sexual," in *Raça e Gênero: Discriminação, Interseccionalidades e Resistênicas*, Beatriz Melo, Monica Pimentel, Silvia Araújo, Simédia Pereira (eds.) (São Paulo: Educ, 2020), 65–88; João Costa Vargas, "Terror sexual é genocídio: o estupro da mulher Negra como elemento estrutural e estruturante da diaspora – por uma análise quilombista da antinegritude," *Revista Latino-Americana de Criminologia* 1, no. 2 (2021): 35–67

CHAPTER 2
PHASES

1 RONDESP, Rondas Especiais, meaning Special Patrols, is a Military Police battalion in charge of engaging heavily armed groups. See an article by Hamilton Borges, "Tão Cruel e sanguinaria quanto o Batalhão de Operações Especiais (BOPE)," *Justiça Global*, February 5, 2015, https://www.global.org.br.

2 Founded in 1948, the OAS is the premier regional organization that provides the hemisphere's main political, juridical, and social governmental forum. See https://www.oas.org/en.

3 Rede de Comunidades e Movimentos contra a Violência, "22 de Junho 2009 (Br-Ba) Massacre de Canabrava, na periferia de Salvador da Bahia," *Passa Palavra*, June 22, 2009, https://passapalavra.info.

4 "Policial Civil é assassinado no final de linha de Canabrava," *Correio*, June 16, 2009, https://www.correio24horas.com.br.

5 For example, in 2007 Rise Up or Die! started the Association of Family and Friends of the Prisoners of the State of Bahia, still active today. See "Public Notice from the Association of Family and Friends of the Prisoners of the State of Bahia (ASFAP-BA)," *Reaja ou Será Morto/Reaja ou Será Morta*, April 22, 2020, https://reajanasruas.blogspot.com.

6 "O Estado Brasileiro no Banco dos Réus," *Blog da Redação*, April 10, 2012, https://outraspalavras.net

CHAPTER 3
FUNDAMENTALS

1 Audre Lorde, "The Uses of Anger: Women Responding to Racism," in *Sister Outsider: Essays and Speeches* (Trumansburg, NY: Crossing Press, 1984), 115–125.

2 Secretaria Nacional de Justiça, "Plano juventude viva: um levantamento histórico," *Atlas das Juventudes*, 2018, https://atlasdasjuventudes.com.br.

3 "Não Vote, Reaja: Movimentos lançam campanha por boicote às eleições," *Periferia em Movimento*, July 11, 2016, https://periferiaemmovimento.com.br. The vote is mandatory in Brazil; refusing to vote is an act of civil disobedience that can lead to legal punishment.

4 Mano Brown, "Sou Função (part. Dexter)," *Letras*, accessed April 30, 2024, https://www.letras.mus.br

5 Capoeira is a martial art, disguised as a drum and dance circle, invented by enslaved Africans in Brazil.

6 "Bahia é o estado mais letal do Nordeste e 100% dos mortos pela polícia em Salvador são negros," *G1*, December 14, 2021, https://g1.globo.com/ba

7   Igor Carvalho, "Juíza declara em sentença que homen negro é criminoso 'em razão de sua raça,'" *Brasil de Fato*, August 12, 2020, https://www.brasildefato.com.br.

8   Lombroso (1835–1909) and Garofalo (1851–1934) were members of the Italian School of criminology, which, based on their understanding of human evolution, considered so-called "born criminals" as members of a human subspecies, or people with arrested development or degeneracy. Lombroso connected criminal behavior to measurable physical traits such as shape and size of the jaw, eyes, ears, nose, etc.

CHAPTER 4
FUTURITY

1   Abdias do Nascimento, "Quilombismo."

2   Beatriz Nascimento, *Uma História Feita por Mãos Negras.*

3   Borges, *Bantu Machine.*

4   During the 2022 presidential election, there were several disturbances on Brazilian freeways enacted by Bolsonaro supporters. For example, see Ana Ionova, Andre Spigriol, Lais Martins and Jack Nicas, "Brazil's election officials demand answers for police stops of buses carrying voters," *New York Times*, October 30, 2022, https://www.nytimes.com.

5   In Afro-Brazilian rituals, the Alabê is the person responsible for playing the atabaque, a tall wooden hand drum.

6   "Proposal" is rooted in Candomblé, as in fulfilling a sacred preordained plan.

7   President Lula's third inauguration took place on January 1st, 2023. See "Lula sworn in as president of divided Brazil amid tight security," *Al Jazeera*, January 1, 2023, https://www.aljazeera.com.

8   On the legal debate on the 1916 Civil Code between Barbosa and Bevilaqua, see Gisele M. Salgado, "Discussões Legislativas do Código

Civil de 1916: Uma Revisão Historiográfica," *Revista Eletrônica da Faculdade de Direito da Universidade Federal do Pelotas* 5, no. 1 (Jan–Jul 2019): 40–84.

9   Eliana Alves Cruz, "Para o homen negro que viveu dentro de Pelé," *Folha de S. Paulo*, December 29, 2022, https://www1.folha.uol.com.br.

10 The manifestos are available on Rise Up's website: https://reajanasruas.blogspot.com

11 Naiara Galarraga Cortázar, "The color of politics in Brazil," *El País*, September 25, 2022, https://english.elpais.com.

12 Ministério do Desenvolvimento e Assistência Social, Família e Combate à Fome, "Fome no Brasil piorou nos últimos três anos, mosta relatório da FAO," *Presidência da República*, July 12, 2023, https://www.gov.br.

AFTERWORD: "POETRY OF INSURRECTION, AESTHETICS OF BLACK AUTONOMY"

1   *Blood in My Eye*, 14.

ABOUT THE AUTHORS

ANDREIA BEATRIZ

A graduate of the Universidade Federal de Ciências da Saúde de Porto Alegre (Federal University of Health Sciences, Porto Alegre), Andreia is a medical doctor with a specialization in Family and Community Medicine obtained at the Sociedade Brasileira de Medicina de Família e Comunidade (Brazilian Society of Family and Community Medicine). She has a Masters and is pursuing a doctoral degree in Collective Health. Between 2021–2024, Andreia was a member of the Conselho Nacional de Política Criminal e Penitenciária (National Council of Criminal and Penitentiary Policy). As a doctor, between 2007 and 2023, she was a member of a health group in the Lemos Brito Penitentiary in Salvador. Since 2008, she is a faculty in the Department of Health and a researcher in the Núcleo Interdisciplinar de Estudos em Desigualdades em Sáude (Interdisciplinary Nucleus for the Study on Health Inequalities) of the Universidade Estadual de Feira de Santana (State University of Feira de Santana). Since 2018, she is the chief faculty of the Programa de Residência em Medicina de Família e Comunidade (Residency Program in Family and Community Medicine) of the Escola Bahiana de Medicina e Saúde Pública (Bahia School of Medicine and Pulic Health). Currently she is a member of the Equipe de Avaliação e Acompanhamento das Medidas Terapêuticas Aplicáveis a Pessoa com Transtorno Mental em Conflito com a Lei (Evaluating and Accompanying Team of the Therapeutic Measures Applicable to People with Mental Disorder while in Conflict with the Law) of the State of Bahia Health Secretariat. Since 2005, as the coordinator of Rise Up or Die!, she helps develop practices and actions for the struggle against the genocide of Black people in the streets, favelas, and inside prisons. She conceptualized the permanent action Saúde e Cultura Intramuros (Health and Culture Between Walls) in the Bahia prison system. Andreia is the author of *Olhar por Entre as Grades, Vidas em Poemas* (2020) and *Tempo em Mim* (2023). She codirected the documentary *Genocídio e Movimentos*, released in 2021 by the production company Couro de Rato.

HAMILTON BORGES DOS SANTOS

Born on the Rua do Curuzu, number 294, in Liberdade, Salvador, state of Bahia, the neighborhood with the greatest concentration of Black people. He stresses that his knowledge comes from the Black movement and his affective relation with the women of his family, particularly his paternal grandmother. In the 1980s, he became a member of the Theater Group of the Sesc-SENAC, in the Pelourinho neighborhood of Salvador, and undertook courses in cooking and theater. He founded the Grupo de Intervenção Poética (the Poetry Intervention Group) os Maloqueiros, which recited Black poetry in the city streets. In 1994, Hamilton relocated to Belo Horizonte, in the state of Minas Gerais, where he founded the theater group Teatro Negro e Atitude (Black Theater and Attitude), which is still active with a Black/African repertoire. In 1996, he coordinated the first Encontro da Juventude Negra e Favelada (Encounter of the Black Youth of the Favelas), which brought together favela youth from all parts of Brazil. As the coordinator of the South and North regional administrations, he worked at Belo Horizonte Secretaria Municipal de Cultura (Municipal Culture Secretariat). Since 2003, when he returned to Salvador, at CEAO, of the Universidade Federal da Bahia (Federal University of Bahia), in the Ceafro Program, he has worked as an educator articulating knowledge of cultural politics. In 2005, he idealized Rise Up or Die! and he's still part of the organization today. With Andreia Beatriz, he coordinated the first, second, third, and fourth International March Against the Genocide of Black People in Brazil. Currently he is active in the Winnie Mandela Pan-Africanist School, focusing on literature, political formation, and cultural communitarian action. With Andreia Beatriz, he is the cofounder of the Agba Eleye Library and the Reaja Editing House. He coordinates the Culture Between Walls Project at the Lemos Brito Penitentiary, where he develops cultural politics actions and struggles for the rights of prisoners. He codirected the documentary "Genocído e Movimentos," released in 2021 by the Couro de Rato production company. He coordinates the Cultural Center Quilombo Xis, as well as the Projeto Literatura Preta Itinerante (The Traveling Black Literature Project): os Novos Quilombos de Zumbi, dedicated to the formation of communitarian cultural agents, and the placement of refrigerators full of books in apartheid communities. Under the Reaja Editing House, Hamilton published *Teoria Geral do Fracasso* (2017), a book of poems; *Salvador, Cidade Túmulo* (2018), a fictional narrative, which was translated into English and released in California and in Washington, DC; *Livro Preto de Ariel* (2019), a romance; *Libido, Dendê e Melanina* (2020), a book of short stories, and *Bantu Madhine: The Man who Wanted to be White* (2023), a romance. He is affiliated to a Quilombista combat literature.

JOÃO H. COSTA VARGAS

Professor of Black Study and Anthropology at the University of California, Riverside and the coauthor of *Antiblackness* (with Moon-Kie Jung, 2021).

ABOUT COMMON NOTIONS

Common Notions is a publishing house and programming platform that fosters new formulations of living autonomy. We aim to circulate timely reflections, clear critiques, and inspiring strategies that amplify movements for social justice.

Our publications trace a constellation of critical and visionary meditations on the organization of freedom. By any media necessary, we seek to nourish the imagination and generalize common notions about the creation of other worlds beyond state and capital. Inspired by various traditions of autonomism and liberation—in the US and internationally, historical and emerging from contemporary movements—our publications provide resources for a collective reading of struggles past, present, and to come.

Common Notions regularly collaborates with political collectives, militant authors, radical presses, and maverick designers around the world. Our political and aesthetic pursuits are dreamed and realized with Antumbra Designs.

www.commonnotions.org
info@commonnotions.org

MORE FROM COMMON NOTIONS

CLAIM NO EASY VICTORIES
THE LEGACY OF AMÍLCAR CABRAL

Firoze Manji and Bill Fletcher, Jr.

Copublished with Daraja Press

FEBRUARY 2024
978-1-942173-84-7
Paperback | 384 pages | 6 x 9 in | $26
Black Radical Tradition | Movement
Building | Decolonization

An anthology of revolutionary, poet, liberation philosopher Amílcar Cabral brings to life the contemporary resonance of his thought for today's freedom movements.

In this unique collection of essays, contemporary thinkers commemorate the anniversary of Cabral's assassination, reflecting on the legacy of this extraordinary individual and his relevance to contemporary struggles for self-determination and emancipation. The book serves both as an introduction, or reintroduction, to one that the rulers and beneficiaries of global racial capitalism would rather see forgotten.

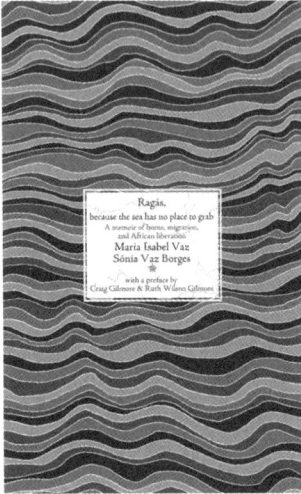

RAGÁS
BECAUSE THE SEA HAS NO PLACE TO GRAB

Maria Isabel Vaz and Sónia Vaz Borges

JUNE 2024
978-1-945335-09-9
Paperback | 160 pages | 5 x 8 in | $18
Colonialism | Migration | Africa

A memoir of a mother and daughter's return to Cabo Verde reveals the legacies of national liberation, a story of memory and migration, and the psychic and physical landscape that colonialism has wrought.

While accompanying her mother, Maria Isabel Vaz, home to Santiago Island, Cabo Verde—a native land she had never been to before—Sónia Vaz Borges conducts research on the history of militant resistance to Portuguese colonialism, of the education initiatives of the African Party for the Independence of Guinea Bissau and Cabo Verde (PAIGC), and the lessons for freedom available for today.

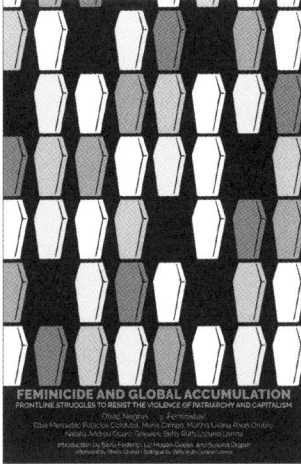

FEMINICIDE AND GLOBAL ACCUMULATION

Otras Negras . . . Y ¡Feministas!, Elba Mercedes Palacios Córdoba, María Mercedes Campo, Martha Liliana Rivas Orobio, Natalia Andrea Ocoró Grajales, Betty Ruth Lozano Lerma

OCTOBER 2021
978-1-942173-44-1
Paperback | 256 pages | 6 x 9 in | $20
Feminism | Latin America | Social Movements

Feminicide and Global Accumulation brings us to the frontlines of an international movement of Black, Indigenous, popular, and mestiza women's organizations fighting against violence—interpersonal, state sanctioned, and economic—that is both endemic to the global economy and the contemporary devalued status of racialized women, trans, and gender non-conforming communities in the Global South.

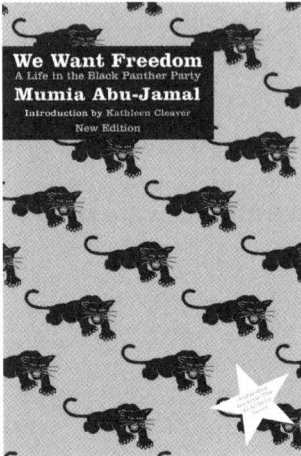

WE WANT FREEDOM

A LIFE IN THE BLACK PANTHER PARTY

Mumia Abu-Jamal
Introduction by Kathleen Cleaver

OCTOBER 2016
978-1-942173-04-5
Paperback | 336 pages | 5 x 8 in | $20
Social Movements | African American
History | Memoir

Mumia Abu Jamal, America's most famous political prisoner, is internationally known for his radio broadcasts and books emerging "Live from Death Row." In his youth Mumia Abu-Jamal helped found the Philadelphia branch of the Black Panther Party, wrote for the national newspaper, and began his life-long work of exposing the violence of the state as it manifests in entrenched poverty, endemic racism, and unending police brutality. In *We Want Freedom*, Mumia combines his memories of day-to-day life in the Party with analysis of the history of Black liberation struggles. The result is a vivid and compelling picture of the Black Panther Party and its legacy.

Applying his poetic voice and unsparing critical gaze, Mumia examines one of the most revolutionary and most misrepresented groups in the US.

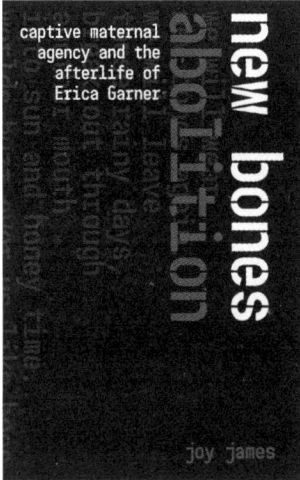

captive maternal
agency and the
afterlife of
Erica Garner

new bones
abolition

joy james

NEW BONES ABOLITION
CAPTIVE MATERNAL AND (AFTER)LIFE OF ERICA GARNER

Joy James

OCTOBER 2023
978-1-942173-74-8
Paperback | 240 pages | 5.5 x 8.5 in | $20
Abolition | Black Radical Tradition |
Feminism

Reflecting on police violence, political movements, Black feminism, Erica Garner, Mumia Abu-Jamal, caretakers and compradors, Joy James analyzes the "Captive Maternal," which emerges from legacies of colonialism, chattel slavery and predatory policing, to explore the stages of communal rebellion that manifest through war resistance. She recognizes a long line of gendered and ungendered freedom fighters, who, within aracialized and economically-stratified democracy, transform from coerced or conflicted caretakers into builders of movements, who realize the necessity of maroon spaces, and ultimately the inevitability of becoming war resisters that mobilize against genocide and state violence.

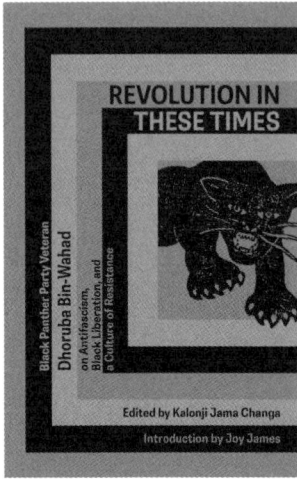

REVOLUTION IN THESE TIMES

Dhoruba Bin-Wahad
Edited by Kalonji Jama Changa
Foreword by Joy James

FEBRUARY 2025
978-1-945335-13-6
Paperback | 256 pages | 6 x 9 in | $20
Black Liberation | Antifascism |
Resistance | Black Panther Party

Revolution in These Times delivers veteran Black Panther Party member, Black Liberation Army leader, and former political prisoner Dhoruba Bin-Wahad direct in his own words to offer us an analysis of how today's resurgent right-wing agenda is an outgrowth of the ongoing and historical political struggle between the oppressed masses and settler-colonialism of America and Europe. Bin-Wahad not only explores how white supremacist politics have recaptured the American imagination but also prescribes a radical grassroots response to counter this ideology and supplant the violent state repression that keeps it in power.

Bin Wahad pieces together fight-back strategies against the police and the state through a process of mobilizing in the streets, on the block, and in our communities, while gathering mass through antifascist coalition-building in a manner unrealized since the 1960s and 1970s. In this series of interviews, Bin Wahad grounds us in the now, seamlessly weaving together firsthand accounts of his own and other's revolutionary past in the history of struggle, alongside lessons for today.

BECOME A COMMON NOTIONS MONTHLY SUSTAINER

These are decisive times ripe with challenges and possibility, heartache, and beautiful inspiration. More than ever, we need timely reflections, clear critiques, and inspiring strategies that can help movements for social justice grow and transform society.

Help us amplify those words, deeds, and dreams that our liberation movements, and our worlds, so urgently need.

Movements are sustained by people like you, whose fugitive words, deeds, and dreams bend against the world of domination and exploitation.

For collective imagination, dedicated practices of love and study, and organized acts of freedom.
By any media necessary.
With your love and support.

Monthly sustainers start at $15 and receive each new book in our publishing program.

commonnotions.org/sustain